The World of Extreme Happiness

Frances Ya-Chu Cowhig's play *Lidless* received the Yale Drama Series Award, an Edinburgh Fringe First Award, the Keene Prize for Literature, and the David Calicchio Emerging American Playwright Prize. In 2011 she was awarded the Wasserstein Prize by the Educational Foundation of America for her most recent work, *The World of Extreme Happiness*, seen in London in autumn 2013 at the National Theatre. Her plays have been produced by the Goodman Theatre (Chicago), Manhattan Theatre Club (New York), Crowded Fire (San Francisco), Trafalgar Studios 2 (London), Page 73 Productions (New York), Interact Theatre (Philadelphia), Borderlands Theatre (Tuscon) and the Contemporary American Theatre Festival (West Virginia). She is currently under commission from Manhattan Theatre Club, the Goodman Theatre and the National Theatre. Frances received a MFA in Writing from the James A. Michener Center for Writers at UT Austin, a BA in Sociology from Brown University, and a certificate in Ensemble-Based Physical Theatre from the Dell'Arte International School of Physical Theatre. Her work has been published by Yale University Press, Glimmer Train, Methuen Drama, Samuel French, and Dramatists Play Service. Frances was born in Philadelphia, and raised in Northern Virginia, Okinawa, Taipei and Beijing.

Frances Ya-Chu Cowhig

The World of Extreme Happiness

second edition

with an afterword by
Joshua Takano Chambers-Letson

B L O O M S B U R Y
LONDON • NEW DELHI • NEW YORK • SYDNEY

Bloomsbury Methuen Drama

An imprint of Bloomsbury Publishing Plc

Imprint previously known as Methuen Drama

50 Bedford Square	1385 Broadway
London	New York
WC1B 3DP	NY 10018
UK	USA

www.bloomsbury.com

BLOOMSBURY, METHUEN DRAMA and the Diana logo
are trademarks of Bloomsbury Publishing Plc

First published 2013
First published in the USA in 2014 with revisions to the script and a new cover

© Frances Ya-Chu Cowhig, 2013, 2014

Frances Ya-Chu Cowhig has asserted her right under the Copyright, Designs
and Patents Act 1988 to be identified as the author of this work.

British Library Cataloguing-in-Publication Data
A catalogue record for this book is available from the British Library

ISBN: PB: 978-1-4742-2770-4
ePDF: 978-1-4742-2773-5
ePub: 978-1-4742-2771-1

Library of Congress Cataloging-in-Publication Data
A catalog record for this book is available from the Library of Congress

Series: Modern Plays

Typeset by Country Setting, Kingsdown, Kent CT14 8ES
Printed and bound in Great Britain

The World of Extreme Happiness

The People, the so-called People, are simple-minded loafers who linger on in any steadily worsening situation, people who have been dulled and forsaken by the deceptions of culture, their personalities deprived and lost, they are people who have abandoned their rights and responsibilities, who walk like ghosts on the ever-widening streets, and whose true emotions, dreams and homes are long lost. They will no longer feel warmth in the night, no longer have expectations, and they shall not dream again.*

* *Ai Weiwei's Blog: Writings, Interviews, and Digital Rants, 2006 –2009*, translated into English by Lee Ambrozy (MIT Press, 2011)

The world premiere of *The World of Extreme Happiness* was produced by Goodman Theatre, Chicago, Illinois (Robert Falls, Artistic Director; Roche Schulfer, Executive Director) and Manhattan Theatre Club, New York, New York (Lynne Meadow, Artistic Director; Barry Grove, Executive Producer). The cast was as follows:

Pete/Ran Feng	Ruy Iskandar
Old Lao/Gao Chen/Mr. Destiny	Francis Jue
James Lin/Li Han	Donald Li
Sunny	Jennifer Lim
Artemis Chang/Wang Hua	Jodi Long
Ming-Ming/Qing Shu Min/Xiao Li	Jo Mei

Director   Eric Ting
Set Designer   Mimi Lien
Costume Designer   Jenny Mannis
Lighting Designer   Tyler Micoleau
Sound Designer   Mikhail Fiksel
Casting by   Adam Belcuore, Nancy Piccione, Kelly Gillespie
Dramaturg   Neena Arndt
Dance Consultant   William Yuekun Wu
Production Stage Manager   Kimberly Osgood

The World of Extreme Happiness received a developmental production in London in The Shed at the National Theatre on 25 September 2013. The cast was as follows:

Xiao Li/Ming-Ming/Qing Shu Min	Vera Chok
Wang Hua/Artemis Chang	Sarah Lam
Sunny	Katie Leung
Ran Feng/Pete/Mr. Destiny	Chris Lew Kum Hoi
Old Lao/Gao Chen	Junix Inocian
Li Han/James Lin	Daniel York

Director Michael Longhurst
Designer Chloe Lamford
Lighting Designer Philip Gladwell
Movement Anna Morrissey
Music and Sound Designers Max and Ben Ringham
Fight Director Bret Yount
Company Voice Work Kate Godfrey

The World of Extreme Happiness was originally commissioned and developed by South Coast Repertory with support from the Elizabeth George Foundation. It was produced in a developmental production by Goodman Theatre, Chicago, in the New Stages Amplified Festival.

Acknowledgements

I am grateful to the following people and institutions who championed *The World of Extreme Happiness* and contributed to its development: Tanya Palmer and Robert Falls at the Goodman Theatre; Kelly Miller and David Emmes at South Coast Rep; Jerry Patch, Annie MacRae and Mandy Greenfield at Manhattan Theatre Club; Amy Mueller at Playwrights Foundation; Ben Power and Nick Hynter at the National Theatre, and the Sundance Institute Retreat at UCROSS.

I am indebted to the friends and family who housed me during the development of this piece: Christopher Chen and Cindy Im, Laurie Parker, Steve, Peg and Jordan Webb, Cecily Parks, Andrea and Peter Yordan.

Thank you also to my amazing theatre agents Antje Oegel and Harriet Pennington-Legh, directors Eric Ting, Michael Longhurst and Jonathan Berry, Anna Brewer at Bloomsbury, David Hare and Francine Horn for their continued advocacy and support, and Joshua Chambers-Letson for the afterword.

Deepest gratitude, as always, to my parents David and Jessie Cowhig for their love and support, and my partner Brian Awehali for his courage, honesty and inspiration. This work is dedicated to them.

Characters

Sunny, *eighteen to twenty, female. Migrant factory worker*

Pete, *sixteen to eighteen, male. Sunny's brother*
ALSO PLAYS **Ran Feng**, *twenty to thirty-six. Coal miner*

Li Han, *twenty-five to forty-five, male. Sunny's father. Coal miner*
ALSO PLAYS **James Lin**, *fifty-one. Factory owner*

Old Lao, *sixty-five, male. Head of Sanitation at Shenzhen Factory*
ALSO PLAYS **Gao Chen**, *fifty. Public Security Officer*

Mr. Destiny, *thirty-three. Self-help guru*

Artemis Chang, *fifty-two, female. Vice President of Price-Smart China*
ALSO PLAYS **Wang Hua**, *forty to sixty. Midwife turned fix-it woman*

Qing Shu Min, *twenty-six, female. Police officer*
ALSO PLAYS **Xiao Li**, *twenty-three. Sunny and Pete's mother*

Ming-Ming, *twenty-three. Factory worker*

Place and time
Rural and urban China, 1992 and 2011–12

Act One

One

Rural China, 1992. A dilapidated brick house in a town along the Yangtze River. **Li Han** *squats by a tin slop-bucket shelling peanuts. He tosses the husks into the bucket. A lit cigarette is perched between his lips. His hands and face are smudged with coal dust.* **Ran Feng** *enters, squats beside* **Li Han**, *and lights a cigarette.*

Ran Feng Put all your love in one basket and you live in fear of losing it.

Li Han Is that why you fuck so many whores?

Ran Feng What if your favorite gets killed by her pimp? What if she hangs herself, or gets pregnant and stops being such a nice fuck? Spread your love in many places, and you will never experience heartbreak.

Li Han Go home.

Ran Feng It's only been a week. Don't lose hope.

Li Han Ever since she left I haven't been able to sleep. I lie awake, thinking of all the possibilities. Evil men . . . Bad weather . . . What if she was kidnapped, or shot down by gangsters? What if I receive a ransom note, strapped to a severed leg?

Ran Feng That only happens in Taiwan.

Li Han Yesterday I dreamed Xin Xin came to my bed and sat on my face. As she rocked back and forth, making soft little sounds, I lay still, savoring her warmth on my skin, weeping fat tears of joy because my heart had come back to me. Suddenly, I felt something hot and gooey slide down my cheek. For a moment, I was confused. Then, I realized Xin Xin had laid a turd between my eyes. It mixed with my tears, slid towards my lips, and melted on my tongue. It was salty, and sweet. Like tofu, fermented with black beans. What do you think that means?

Ran Feng   It means you've lost the love of your life.

Li Han   Because the turd was still warm?

Ran Feng   Li Han. She shat on your face.

Li Han   That could mean she was relaxed. Happy to see me. Maybe –

Ran Feng (*interrupting*)   Li Han. She shat on your face, and you ate it. The symbolism's obvious. You accepted shit into your mouth and digested it.

Li Han   It could be a good omen. What if it means –

Ran Feng   If your beloved bird doesn't make it home, I'll give you the offspring of my best breeding pair and you can find your heart all over again.

Li Han   I don't want your second-rate pigeon. I want Xin Xin! If she's not back by evening I'll die in my sleep from heartbreak.

Ran Feng *and* **Li Han** *continue to smoke and shell peanuts. Lights come up in the next room, where* **Wang Hua** *assists* **Xiao Li** *through the final stages of labor.*

Xiao Li (*screaming*)   Get out of me you son of a turtle!

Wang Hua   Push!

Xiao Li   Get out before you crush my guts!

Wang Hua   Harder!

Xiao Li (*through pushes*)   For nine months you've been eating me like a plague. Robbing my breath. Stealing my blood. (*Gasps.*) Fuccck!

She doubles over, moaning. **Wang Hua** *rubs her swollen belly.*

Wang Hua   Come out, baby. You have a nice house, and a pretty mom, even though she has the mouth of a farmer.

Xiao Li (*to* **Wang Hua**)   Fuck your mother.

Wang Hua   It's crowning!

Xiao Li   Does it have balls?

Wang Hua   PUSH!

Xiao Li (*through pushes*)   What. Is. IT?!

Wang Hua   Xiao Li, scream with me. With each scream, push harder, stand taller. Shoot the baby towards the ground.

They scream together, a series of groans, shouts and moans.

Xiao Li (*screaming*)   Get out!

Wang Hua   Say something nice!

Xiao Li   The sky is blue the water's clean you can crawl and never get dirty!

Wang Hua   Don't lie!

Xiao Li   You can be the first son and cherished heir. Everything we have will be yours!

Wang Hua   One more push!

Xiao Li   Aiighhiyiyiiyiyiyiyiyahyuhhhhh!

Wang Hua *catches the baby as it comes out.*

Wang Hua   It's done.

Xiao Li   How does his penis look?

Wang Hua *checks the baby's genitals then wraps it in newspaper and tucks it under her arm.*

Wang Hua   Get some rest.

Xiao Li   Sometimes you can't tell. The balls hide in the stomach, and you –

Wang Hua (*interrupting*)   Shut up before you get us in trouble.

Xiao Li   You said that if I ate more meat –

Wang Hua   It's not that simple.

Xiao Li   I can't read. I can't just look in a book and find instructions.

Wang Hua   You want the recipe for boy babies? Lose weight, comb your hair, and get your husband to fuck you. You must have been very bad in your last life to be punished so much in this one.

Xiao Li   I want a son.

Wang Hua   Don't waste your breath wanting. Just make one.

Xiao Li (*screaming*)   I want a son!

Wang Hua *approaches* **Li Han** *and* **Ran Feng**. **Li Han** *lifts the lid off the slop bucket.* **Wang Hua** *drops the newspaper bundle inside.* **Li Han** *hacks a loogie, spits into the slop bucket, and replaces the lid.*

Wang Hua   Make a soup with flour and water. She'll need it to regain her strength.

Li Han   I paid for a son.

Wang Hua   My job is to deliver a child.

Li Han   A boy is a child. A girl is a thing. Five times I've paid for a child. Five times you've given me things.

Wang Hua   It must be fate that all the Li family deserves is things.

Li Han *slaps* **Wang Hua**. *She staggers backwards, pulls a wad of bills out of her pocket and throws them at* **Li Han**.

Li Han   One more 'thing' and you'll never work this village again.

Wang Hua *kicks* **Ran Feng**. *Peanuts fly across the floor.* **Li Han** *lights a cigarette.*

Ran Feng   Ma! What the fuck was that for?

Wang Hua   You watch your mother get hit and do nothing?

Ran Feng   Next time don't give him a girl.

Wang Hua   Get up. Grow up. Find a wife.

She spits at **Li Han**'*s feet, then exits.* **Ran Feng** *follows her out.* **Xiao Li** *whimpers in the next room.*

Li Han   The neighbors are mocking us. If we don't have a son, we'll be the laughing stock of the village. Try harder, okay? The fate of seven generations rests on us.

He lifts the slop bucket and heads for the door.

Xiao Li   Three months she's been kicking. She was so fierce. So demanding.

Li Han *doesn't respond. He is frozen by the front door, listening to something.*

Xiao Li   Why would a girl do such things?

Li Han   Do you hear that?

Xiao Li   Hear what?

Li Han   That sound. That beautiful, precious sound.

He opens the front door. He gasps in delight, and crouches by the door.

My heart! You've come back! Oh no, a broken wing? You must have hopped home, you poor thing. Don't worry. Daddy will fix you up.

He scoops up the unseen bird and carries her to an offstage pigeon loft.

Li Han *(offstage)*   Xiao Li! Perfect Girl needs a treat.

Xiao Li   The pig needs to eat.

Li Han *(offstage)*   Have some mercy. She's suffering!

Xiao Li   Look in the slop bucket. There might be some yam scrapings.

Li Han *enters and lifts the lid off the slop bucket.*

Li Han *(screams)*   Aughyiyaiiyah!

Xiao Li   What?

Li Han   It's still alive! And – fuck me! It's smiling!

Xiao Li   Foolish girl. Tell her to die.

Li Han   She's smiling, like I'm the sun on a cold winter day! I've never seen such a pathetic thing.

Xiao Li   Close the lid. She'll die soon enough.

Li Han   What if this is a good omen?

Xiao Li   Horse shit. Girls are bad luck.

Li Han *scoops the soggy newspaper bundle out of the slop bucket and places it into* **Xiao Li***'s arms.*

Li Han (*chuckling*)   Look at that. Born into a bucket of pig slop, and she's smiling like a Buddha. We'll name her Sunny. Heheh.

Xiao Li   I want a son.

Li Han   Then make one.

He pulls yam scraps from the bucket, then heads to the pigeon loft.

Li Han   Nurse her. Keep her soft. We'll sell her once she's old enough to fuck.

(*To pigeon.*) Here you go, my beauty.

Xiao Li (*to bundle in her arms*)   Stupid girl.

Li Han (*offstage*)   Who's the prettiest birdie?

Xiao Li   Why are you alive? And still smiling?

Li Han (*offstage*)   Who loves you so much?

Xiao Li   Don't you know the lives of girls are full of misery?

Li Han (*offstage*)   Daddy loves his Perfect Girl. Yes he does.

Xiao Li (*to baby*)   Once upon a time, on a Mountain of Flowers and Fruit, a pregnant rock released a stone egg, from which hatched the King of the Monkeys. He found a teacher and learned the Seventy-Two Transformations, so he could change into any form. (*Beat.*) Sunny Li. Drink.

Xiao Li *lifts the newspaper bundle to her breast.* **Sunny** (*eighteen*) *enters, wearing a factory uniform. The next scene assembles around her.*

Two

Shenzhen, 2011. Factory bathroom. **Sunny** *mops the floor. Her cell phone, which has a techno-pop ringtone, goes off. She attaches an earpiece and continues mopping.*

Sunny *(into phone)* What?

Pete, *wearing his school uniform, does acrobatic warm-ups and stretches inside the dilapidated brick house in rural China where* **Sunny** *was born. He is on the phone.*

Pete *(into phone)* "Pigsy looked at Monkey and said – "

Sunny "Brother, I'll credit you with all kinds of transformations, but this type of thing is beyond you."

Pete *performs the next section in the voice and mannerisms of the Monkey King.*

Pete " 'Not at all,' replied Monkey. 'Chop off my arms, and I can still strike. Hack off my legs, and I can still walk. Rip out my heart and I will mysteriously recover. I'll bathe in boiling oil and come out cleaner than I went in.' "

Li Han *enters, covered in coal dust and stripped down to white boxers.*

Pete *(into phone)* Ba's home.

He pours hot water into a basin of water for **Li Han**, *who steps in and washes soot off his body.* **Sunny** *continues mopping.*

Li Han Too hot.

Pete *pours cold water into the basin.* **Li Han** *continues washing.*

Sunny Guess what?

Pete Monkey Butt.

Sunny My section manager jumped out the window.

Pete You told me that last month.

Sunny That was someone else.

Pete Did you see it?

Sunny (*meaning no*)   It was during night shift.

Pete *hands* **Li Han** *a jar of tea. He takes a sip.*

Li Han   Too cold.

He dumps the tea in the bathwater.

Sunny   What did you learn in school?

Pete   Ba thinks I should stop going.

Sunny   Put him on.

Pete *hands* **Li Han** *the phone.*

Sunny   We had a deal.

Li Han   He made it to tenth grade. Enough. He'll get stuck up if he goes further.

Sunny   I paid his tuition.

Li Han   Get a refund. The house needs a new roof.

Sunny   I send you money every month.

Li Han *steps out of the tub, then hacks a loogie into the water.*

Li Han   It's not enough.

Sunny   Stop spending so much on your birds.

Li Han *hangs up the phone, hands it to* **Pete** *and continues washing, with* **Pete**'s *assistance.* **Sunny** *mops the floor furiously.* **Li Han** *towels off, then puts on a ratty T-shirt and loose cotton pants. He pulls a few cabbage leaves from the slop bucket and exits towards the pigeon loft.* **Pete** *calls* **Sunny**. *She answers.*

Sunny   You're staying in school.

Pete   I'll work in the mine. It'll be fun. I'll make my own money and buy what I want.

Sunny   They collapse all the time. Workers who don't die from being crushed cough out their lungs and drown in their own blood.

Pete   Then come home.

Sunny   No.

Pete   If you don't, I'll work in the mines, drink beer for breakfast and spend all my money on hookers and cigarettes.

Sunny   Don't cry to me when your 'friend' falls off and you're dying of AIDS, Black Lung and Hepatitis C.

Pete   No one's going to promote you. You can't read. Everyone knows you're a dirty hick and wants to throw rocks at you, spit on your hair, piss on your shoes, flick boogers down your shirt and thinks you're the stupidest person on earth.

Sunny   Why can't I read? Why am I stupid? Who promised to tutor me whenever I'm home for New Year's? I'm not moving back. It's ugly. Everyone's trapped.

She starts to hang up.

Pete   "There are two methods of escape. Which would you like to learn? The trick of the Heavenly Ladle gives you Thirty-Six Transformations. But the trick of the Earthly Conclusion – that's Seventy-Two Transformations."

He cups his hands around the phone and chants gibberish into it, casting a spell.

Sunny   Shut up and be glad you were born with a penis.

Old Lao, *a grizzled man sporting thick black glasses, a baseball cap and a green uniform enters, carrying a thick binder.* **Sunny** *puts away the earpiece and mops diligently.* **Old Lao** *looks around, making notes and checking things off.*

Pete   Now . . . change.

Pete *and the countryside disappear. A long silence, as* **Sunny** *tries and fails to get* **Old Lao**'s *attention. Finally, she coughs.*

Old Lao   Stay away from me if you're sick. I don't have time to catch cold.

He turns to leave.

Sunny (*hesitant*)   Excuse me. I . . . um . . . I don't mean to trouble you, but – I wanted to know if . . . maybe you would consider . . .

Old Lao (*barks*)   What?

Sunny   Bleach!

Old Lao   What about it?

Sunny   I've been uh . . . using it on toilets – but sometimes it doesn't work.

Old Lao   I bet you're talking about these girl bathrooms. Women have terrible aim. We men know how to shoot straight but you squatting bitches piss all over the place. In the men's room you know what you're getting. Worst-case scenario some guy's got the squirts and there's chunks of chili caked to the pots, but with women – if you're not picking bloody pads off the floor you're mopping up period drips. It's like walking through a war zone. If the bleach isn't working your solution lacks strength. Triple the concentration and leave it on for an hour. That should do the trick.

He returns to his binder.

Sunny   That's . . . good . . . advice. Thank you.

Old Lao   I've been in the sanitation business for fifty years. I know a thing or two about cleaning.

Sunny   I heard one of your section managers – had a bad accident.

Old Lao   If you call jumping out an eight-story window an accident. Spoiled brat. If he thinks this job is hard he should see the public toilets I cleaned in the eighties.

Sunny   He was an only child. I raised my little brother. I'm not spoiled. I know how to work.

Old Lao *starts to exit.*

Sunny   I'd like to – apply for the . . . open management position.

Old Lao   I'd like to fuck every phone girl in the front office and see who screams loudest.

Sunny   I'd appreciate this opportunity.

Old Lao   I'd appreciate a trip to Paris.

Sunny   I need to make more money.

Old Lao   I need to be a rich American. Then, when my legs break down, and I can't hear music, taste meat or smell bread it won't matter – because I live in a big house full of girls dressed like bunny rabbits. (*Sighs.*) Maybe in the next life our dreams will come true.

Sunny   You're unit manager. If you wanted to promote me, you could.

Old Lao   How old are you?

Sunny   Eighteen.

Old Lao   How long have you worked here?

Sunny   Four years.

Old Lao   There are men in this factory who've cleaned toilets for decades. What message would it send if I chose you over them? They'd all jump out the window at once and I'd be stuck scraping guts off the sidewalk. Know what you need to do?

Sunny   What?

Old Lao   Keep your aspirations low and your expectations even lower. That way you'll never be disappointed. Focus on life's little delights. For example – are you listening?

Sunny   Yes!

Old Lao   When I need to take a piss I wait. For at least thirty minutes.

Sunny   Why?

Old Lao   Because then, for the twenty seconds I'm pissing, it feels like the greatest thing I've ever experienced! Want another pearl of wisdom?

Sunny   Uh . . . sure.

Old Lao   Save up for big pleasures. If I can afford a girl every season, the memory of my last fuck keeps me working hard, saving up for the next.

Sunny *mops the floor furiously, trying to hide her disappointment.*

Sunny   Thank you for the help. I'll strengthen my solution and see if it works.

Old Lao   So you knew him.

Sunny   Who?

Old Lao   The kid who jumped out of Building Seven.

Sunny   He was my section manager.

Old Lao   Did he try any funny stuff?

Sunny   Funny stuff? Like what?

Old Lao   Did he try to make you believe something strange, join a cult or sign your name on some papers?

Sunny   No.

Old Lao   How about with other workers? Did you ever see him making – you know . . . (*He makes an ambiguous gesture.*)

Sunny   Huh?

Old Lao (*mumbles so it's unintelligible*)   Political speeches.

Sunny   What?

Old Lao *thrusts a wrinkled document into* **Sunny***'s hand.*

Sunny   What's this?

Old Lao   How should I know? I've never seen it before in my life.

Sunny   But you just –

Old Lao   You say you found it in the bushes, by Building Seven? Looks like the poor kid was in over his head. Good thing you got to it before the police did, or his parents would be extra heartbroken.

Sunny   What are all these signatures?

Old Lao   Sounds like trouble.

Sunny   Did you sign it?

Old Lao   Do I look like a guy that signs political documents?

Sunny   This is a political document?

Old Lao   It is?

Sunny   This is a petition, isn't it?

Old Lao   A petition?! Keep that away from me.

Sunny   But you just –

Old Lao (*interrupts*)   Sorry, kid I can't promote you. Come back in ten years, and I'll see what I can do.

He walks away, leaving **Sunny** *alone with the document.*

Three

An urban loft in Shenzhen. **James Lin** *and* **Artemis Chang** *gaze out of a high-rise window. Both are well dressed,* **James** *in a suit,* **Artemis** *in heels and a designer dress, her hair in an elegant up-do.*

James   Forty years ago this wasn't a Special Economic Zone. It was just dirt, rice, and country people. More people work in my factory than ever lived in our village, over every generation. On days it's not foggy I can see where your family's house used to be.

Artemis   Times change. Every person has to decide – adapt or become obsolete. Isn't that what you used to tell me?

James   I always wanted to be at your place because it was so much nicer than ours. Your grandfather's maps were amazing.

Artemis   You've had too much wine.

James   We were kids down there. Flying kites, running barefoot –

Artemis   If you insist on nostalgia, I'm leaving.

James   I miss the old days.

Artemis   You miss insanity.

James   Life was simple. I couldn't leave the house without running into friends and family.

Artemis   Poor James. Everything's gotten so complicated.

James   Fewer friends – less family –

Artemis   More money . . .

James   For how long? If I don't fix my PR problem I'll lose my foreign investments and be the laughing stock of Shenzhen.

Artemis *unbuttons* **James***' collar and removes his tie.*

Artemis   To the continued partnership of Price-Smart and Jade River Manufacturing.

James   May we keep customers happy, shareholders satisfied –

Artemis   And your workers from committing suicide.

James *walks away, upset by her directness.*

Artemis   What's the matter? Is the jade flute getting clogged?

James   What if it's not about the money? What if my workers just need better beliefs?

Artemis *takes off her earrings and lets down her hair.*

Artemis   We'll fix this. Relax. *(About his unsexy behavior.)* A little impatience spoils great plans.

James   An ignorant man follows public opinion.

Artemis   What kind of beliefs?

James   Suicide rates are lower among Latin American workers. They have heaven to look forward to. Chinese workers have to die, be reborn and suffer all over again.

Artemis   "Price-Smart responds to spate of worker suicides by promising rewards in heaven in exchange for low-wage toil on earth?"

James   Don't just shut me down.

Artemis   Follow the example of Fox-Conn and ask them to sign a no-suicide pledge.

James   The factory isn't the problem. The problem is how the Western press sees us.

Artemis *removes James' suit jacket.*

Artemis   Fine. Let's fix the media message.

James   Rural people have fewer rights. They come to the city, work for me, their lives get better, but when a few fall through the cracks it's my fault?

Artemis   You're saying your factory's a sanctuary?

James   Where my workers have the opportunity to flourish, all expenses paid!

Artemis   It's like one of those reality shows. Young people come from all over, live together and fight to make their lives better.

James   But it's real – and hard. Not a fantasy.

Artemis   How about we make a documentary?

James   A documentary?

Artemis *removes her underwear, leaving her dress on.*

Artemis   About your factory. A never-before-seen look at the hopes and dreams of young migrants who flood cities in search of better opportunities . . . . Compelling factory owners to employ great numbers of the rural poor. Giving them the opportunity to flourish inside a system of rural-urban apartheid.

James   We're talking about eleven suicides in the past month. You really think you can spin that?

Artemis   Suicides happen in clusters. All we're seeing are the problems of similarly sized cities.

James   We could have a high-profile premiere in Beijing. Invite big foreign investors.

Artemis   Diplos and press too. Get one of your workers to speak at the premiere. Reporters love 'rags to riches' stories.

James *moves towards* **Artemis** *to kiss her.*

James   A nation treasures its scholars.

Artemis   She who is drowned is not troubled by rain.

She dodges **James***' kiss and leads him into the bedroom.*

Four

Shenzhen factory, morning. **Sunny** *cleans a bathroom.* **Ming-Ming,** *a factory worker, enters. She wears a robe over her pajamas and carries her toothpaste and toothbrush in a toiletries bucket that has been decoupaged with photographs of* **Artemis Chang***. She doesn't notice* **Sunny***.*

Ming-Ming (*to herself*)   I am the most important person in the world. The things I say and do are important. They are full of meaning. If I wait for success I will fail. Action is the only worthwhile thing.

She takes a portable cassette recorder out of her pocket and presses 'play.' She listens to the recording and mimes corresponding hand motions while brushing her teeth. **Sunny** *continues mopping, but eyes her curiously.*

Tape Recording (*voice of* **Mr. Destiny**)   When shaking hands with a potential employer, first wipe your hand on your clothing to remove any sweat. Failure comes when the palm is clammy. A successful handshake lasts for at least three seconds, but never more than seven. If you hold on for too long you will give the impression of being needy. If you want someone to connect with you, mirror their body language back to them. Avoid doing this with people below you, lest they take it as an invitation to climb to your level. Mimicking people above you on the social ladder increases your chances of being noticed by seventy-nine percent. (*Chimes sound.*) Please assume your Personal Power Position and announce your mantra of the week. (*Chimes sound.*)

Ming-Ming *assumes her Personal Power Position.*

Ming-Ming   "It is my destiny to make lots of money." (*Coaching herself.*) Louder. More conviction. "It is my destiny to MAKE LOTS OF MONEY." (*Coaching herself.*) Push. Dig. Triumph. "IT IS MY DESTINY TO MAKE LOTS OF MONEY!" (*Coaching herself.*) Good improvement. Consolidate your gains.

She holds her hands in prayer and seals it with a loud "OM". **Sunny** *clasps her hands in prayer, mimicking her, accidentally dropping her mop in the process. It crashes to the floor, startling* **Ming-Ming**, *who shrieks and whirls around.*

Ming-Ming   Have you been here this whole time?

Sunny   Yes. What's this?

Sunny *does* **Ming-Ming***'s Personal Power Position.* **Ming-Ming** *flosses her teeth.*

Ming-Ming   That's my Personal Power Position. It fills me with courage, conviction and strength.

Sunny   For what?

Ming-Ming   How do we act around city people?

Sunny   Who?

Ming-Ming   Peasants.

Sunny   Like we're small . . . and stupid.

Ming-Ming   We think we're second-class citizens. And because we believe it, it becomes our reality. Action molds character. Character creates destiny.

Sunny   So when you do your Personal Power Position and say your –

Ming-Ming   Mantra of the week.

Sunny   What happens?

Ming-Ming   It reroutes the circuits of my brain and brings me two steps closer to changing my fate. Try it.

Sunny   I'm on duty.

Ming-Ming   No one controls your brain. You can clean tile *and* change your fate.

Sunny (*while mopping*)   It is my destiny to make lots of money.

Ming-Ming   Louder.

Sunny   It is my destiny to make lots of money!

Ming-Ming   More conviction.

Sunny   It is my destiny to make lots of money!

Ming-Ming   Again.

Sunny   IT IS MY DESTINY TO MAKE LOTS OF MONEY.

Ming-Ming   Try harder.

Sunny   IT IS MY DESTINY TO MAKE LOTS OF MONEY!

Ming-Ming   Don't waste my time.

Sunny   IT IS MY DESTINY TO MAKE LOTS OF MONEY!

Ming-Ming   Disgraceful.

Sunny (*top of her lungs*)   IT IS MY DESTINY TO MAAAKE LOTS OF MOOONNEEEY!

Ming-Ming   You just lit a dead part of your brain and activated some junk DNA.

Sunny   Where did you learn this?

Ming-Ming   It's homework, for a self-help class I take each evening.

Sunny   You work a twelve-hour shift then go to school afterwards?

Ming-Ming   It's like Aristotle said – excellence is a habit. We are what we do. Besides. It's fun! When you finish the course you get a framed diploma from any university you want.

Sunny (*pointing to toiletry bucket*)   Who's that?

Ming-Ming   This brave woman is vice president of the company that sells everything we make in this factory. She was born in the countryside but went to Harvard and Beijing University. Artemis Chang is living proof that we can climb the ladder of success and realize our dreams.

Sunny's *cell phone goes off. She silences it.* **Ming-Ming** *starts to leave.*

Sunny   Can I take the class with you?

Ming-Ming   What makes you think you have what it takes?

Sunny   Because . . . because I believe that I do! And when I believe it, it becomes my reality.

Ming-Ming   A parrot can quote my words back to me. That doesn't make her worthy.

Sunny   Can a parrot pay you fifty kuai?

Ming-Ming   Ninety.

Sunny   Thirty.

Ming-Ming   Sixty.

Sunny   Fifty-five.

Ming-Ming   Meet me by the north gate at 6:40. Don't be late.

Sunny   I won't. Thank you.

Ming-Ming   Thank yourself. You just made your dreams come true.

She exits. **Sunny** *tries her Personal Power Position.*

Five

Li Han's *rural home. Night.* **Pete** *cleans bamboo pigeon-training baskets.* **Li Han** *holds one of his pigeons and inspects its eyes, feet and wings.*

Pete   One-eye cold.

Li Han   Treatment?

Pete   Spit in the offending eye – puh! Then feed her oranges for breakfast.

Li Han   Heaving in nest, sad eyes, no appetite.

Pete   Then she is egg-bound.

Li Han   Cause?

Pete   Sudden heartbreak.

Li Han   Reason?

Pete   Separation from mate. Oil vent, massage stomach in a downward direction.

A beat. **Li Han** *coos at his caged pigeon.*

Li Han   Crusty skin, wobbly walk, pus oozing around new feathers?

Long pause.

Pete   Ba, I have homework.

Li Han *continues to interact with the pigeon.*

Li Han   Check on the birds.

Pete *exits.* **Li Han** *caresses his pigeon, and sings the love song "My Heart Will Go On."* **Wang Hua** *approaches his front door, pulling her fix-it cart, a portable workshop filled with tools and half-mended household artifacts. A greasy tarp covers half the cart. She wears a heavy apron and fingerless gloves.*

Wang Hua   Li Han? Are you home?

Li Han *opens the door but doesn't let her in. He puts the pigeon in one of the training baskets.*

Li Han   It's late.

Wang Hua   I delivered a mended pot to your neighbor and thought I'd stop by.

Li Han   I'm tired.

Wang Hua   I can't charge as much to mend a pan as I could to birth a boy, but I get by. Besides – my hands are too shaky for that other business, and fixing pots is easier on the heart. (*Sighs.*) It's a shame we couldn't save your wife during her final birth. Making a boy took all the strength she had left on earth.

Li Han   Let's talk another time.

Wang Hua   Remember my son, Ran Feng? He went to Shanghai and found work on a construction site.

Li Han   That's a good job.

Wang Hua   It would be – if he kept his head down! The bosses take advantage of the workers. They work eighteen-hour days. Mealtimes and toilet breaks are docked from their pay. It's what we old people expect, but I raised an idiot. (*Whispers.*) He's organizing a strike.

Li Han   Goodnight, Auntie.

Wang Hua   Talk sense into him. Help him see the big picture.

Li Han   Goodnight.

Wang Hua *pulls the greasy tarp off her cart, revealing* **Ran Feng**. *His hands and feet are tied together, a strip of duct tape covers his mouth. He is fast asleep.*

Li Han   Ran Feng?

Wang Hua   He's my only son. He doesn't have a wife to talk sense into him.

She pours a bottle of water onto **Ran Feng***'s face. His eyes fly open. He struggles to free his limbs and mouth but is clumsy and extremely groggy.*

Ran Feng *(through gag)*   Hugggghh? Whaaaaa??

Li Han   He's drugged.

Wang Hua   Listen up, bastard. Li Han has something to say to you!

Ran Feng *(gagged)*   Whuut arrr yuuuu duink mahhhh? Whaaaat duh hellh?

Wang Hua   Go ahead. Tell him!

Li Han   Tell him what?

Ran Feng *(gagged)*   Tellll mee whatuh?

Wang Hua   Tell him why you shouldn't protest! Tell him about the consequences!

Ran Feng *(gagged)*   Fuuuughhht yuuuuu mahhh! Fuuuuugck yuuuu!

Li Han   Tell him yourself.

Ran Feng *(gagged)*   Li Huhannn! Li Huhann! Huellpp!

Wang Hua   I don't have direct experience. Why would he listen?

Ran Feng *(gagged)*   Huellpuh!

Ran Feng *struggles to free himself.*

Li Han   Get. Out.

Wang Hua   Tell him about your brother.

Li Han   I don't have a brother.

Wang Hua   Tell him why you don't!

Li Han   Go home.

Ran Feng (*gagged*)   Yaaah mahh! Ets goh hohme!

Li Han *silently cleans pigeon baskets.*

Wang Hua   Your wife told me what happened when you went to Beijing after June fourth. And how you behaved for months after.

Li Han   . . .

Wang Hua   Silent. Sleeping on straw. In that loft. With his birds.

Li Han   . . .

Wang Hua   I never told Xiao Li, but I knew your grief was the reason she couldn't make sons.

Li Han *coughs, hacks into the slop bucket, then takes the pigeon baskets and heads to the pigeon loft.*

Wang Hua   Please, Li Han! Tell him not to protest.

Li Han   Don't protest.

He exits.

Ran Feng (*gagged*)   Wuuhhgd duh hellll mah!? Wahh deh fuggggh?

Wang Hua   You heard him! Don't protest. Don't protest!!

She smacks **Ran Feng**, *covers him with the greasy tarp, grabs the handles of her pull-cart and exits.*

Six

Shenzhen auditorium, night. **Sunny** *and* **Ming-Ming** *stand together, dressed in aspirational office-worker clothing. They have different hairstyles than before. Unseen around them are thousands of other peasants, who, with* **Ming-Ming**, *are the voices listed as "Unison."*

Unison (*chant*)   Wealth. Wealth. Wealth. Wealth. Power. Power. Power. Power. Fame. Fame. Fame. Fame. Honor. Honor. Honor. Honor.

Announcer (*offstage*)   Ladies and gentlemen, presenting . . . The One . . . The Only . . . Mr. . . . DESTINY!

Mr. Destiny *enters, dressed in faux-Victorian attire. He carries a cordless microphone. The crowd roars.*

Mr. Destiny   What do you deserve?

Unison   Money!

Mr. Destiny   When do you need it?

Unison   Now!

Mr. Destiny   What do you have?

Unison   Power!

Mr. Destiny   When will you use it?

Unison   Now!

Mr. Destiny   Two, four, six, eight −

Unison   Now's the time to change our fate!

Mr. Destiny   Three, six, nine, eleven −

Unison   We will make this life our heaven!

Mr. Destiny   Eight, seven, six, five −

Unison   It is time to feel alive!

Mr. Destiny   Seven, eight, nine, ten −

Unison   We will not be crushed again!

Mr. Destiny   Wealth!

Unison   Honor!

Mr. Destiny   Fame!

Unison   Power!

Mr. Destiny   Who gives you the strength you need?

Unison   With Mr. Destiny we will succeed!

Mr. Destiny   Who helps you live the dreams of your heart?

Unison   With Mr. Destiny our future starts!

Thunderous applause.

Mr. Destiny   Is there anyone new in this house tonight?
Anyone desperate to change their life?

Ming-Ming *nudges* **Sunny**. *She shakes her head, embarrassed.*

Mr. Destiny   If not now, when? How will you change your
life if you can't admit your needs to friends?

Ming-Ming   Raise your hand.

Sunny   I just want to watch.

Mr. Destiny   This is the chance! This is the test!

Ming-Ming   A city person would reach for this opportunity,
take it, and never look back.

Mr. Destiny   You have the power to Change Your Life. All
you need to do is Raise Your Hand!

Ming-Ming *grabs* **Sunny**'s *hand and raises it.*

Sunny   Stop! Please! I'm not

Mr. Destiny   You in the back! What's your name?

A spotlight lands on **Sunny**.

Ming-Ming   Say your name.

Sunny   He's not talking to me.

Ming-Ming   Say it!

Sunny   Sunny Li.

Ming-Ming   Louder!

Sunny   SUNNY LI!

Mr. Destiny　Let's hear it for Sunny Li, for taking her life into her own hands!

Thunderous applause.

Unison (*chanting*)　SUNNY! SUNNY! SUNNY! SUNNY!

The crowd continues to chant as **Ming-Ming** *pushes* **Sunny** *towards* **Mr. Destiny**.

Mr. Destiny　Tell us, Sunny, what brought you here tonight?

Ming-Ming　You want a promotion.

Sunny (*softly*)　I want a promotion.

Ming-Ming　They can't hear you.

Sunny (*louder*)　I want a promotion!

Mr. Destiny　Do you want a promotion, or do you *need* a promotion?

Sunny　I *need* a promotion.

Thunderous applause.

Mr. Destiny　And why do you need a promotion?

Sunny *turns to* **Ming-Ming** *for help.*

Ming-Ming　You deserve it.

Sunny　Because I deserve it!

Mr. Destiny　What else?

Sunny　I want . . . no, I *need* to – move up in the world. Higher and higher. And make more money and have more power.

Mr. Destiny　What will you do with that money and power?

Sunny　Spend it! And get more power! And buy nice things and a good education for me and my brother.

Mr. Destiny　Say more.

Sunny   Then I'll go back to the countryside and laugh at everyone who's still poor . . . and living in dirt. Then I'll move back to the city, buy an apartment, improve myself, memorize every story about the Monkey King and Get Even Stronger!

Unison (*chanting*)   Wealth. Power. Fame. Honor. Wealth. Power. Fame. Honor –

Mr. Destiny   Quiet!

A hush descends. A cordless microphone appears near **Sunny**. *She takes it.*

Mr. Destiny   Okay, Sunny. We're listening. Tell us your sad story.

Sunny (*to* **Ming-Ming**)   My what?

Mr. Destiny   Something is holding you back. Something is keeping you from getting that promotion – and it's not something out here – it's inside you. What is that thing, that memory, that's holding you hostage to your negative feelings?

Sunny   I don't know.

Mr. Destiny   It happened when you were young. It happened before you could defend yourself. That day, something broke inside you, and even today makes you think that you're worthless. That you don't deserve the air you breathe.

Loud booing.

Tell your friends what happened. Get that shame, that burden, off your chest. Let it out, and be free forever.

Sunny (*long silence*)   I can't.

Mr. Destiny   Sunny Li. Why do you like stories about the Monkey King?

Sunny   Because he can change. Into anything.

Mr. Destiny   Monkey hatches from a rock. He's given the power of Seventy-Two Changes then steals immortality, angering the Emperor, who traps him under a mountain. Five centuries later he's freed by a goddess. He befriends a monk and joins his friends on a quest for enlightenment. Sunny Li –

we are those friends. This is that quest. Your task in this
moment is to SPEAK!

Long silence. **Ming-Ming** *grasps* **Sunny***'s hand and squeezes it.*

Sunny   When I was born my parents threw me in a bucket
of pig slop and left me there to die.

Loud booing.

I survived, then my mother died giving birth to my brother.
I had to take care of him – and the house – and vegetables
and chickens and pig. I wanted school, but we were too poor
until I came to the city and found work in the factory. Now
he's a student but all I've learned is how to bleach toilets and
scrub floors.

Mr. Destiny   Sunny Li believes she was born into a bucket
of pig slop. She never feels good enough. She eats less than
her share at dinner. She dresses so no one will notice her.
Some days she wonders whether anyone would care if she
disappeared altogether.

Sunny   How did you know that? How did you –

Mr. Destiny (*interrupting*)   I'm here to tell you that bucket of
pig slop never happened. When you were born your mother
hugged you and thanked the heavens for your birth. She kissed
you all over, rubbed sesame oil into your skin, massaged your
hands and feet and said – "Welcome to the world, Sunny.
You're exactly what I wanted. I'm so happy to finally meet you."

Sunny   She didn't want me. The only reason I lived was –

Mr. Destiny   Forget who you were. Imagine who you can
be in another time – like this one. In another place – like the
one you're standing in. If you were speaking to that new
Sunny now, would you want her to think she was born into a
bucket of pig slop?

Sunny   No.

Mr. Destiny   What would you want her to believe?

Sunny   That she was loved. And wanted.

Mr. Destiny   Just like you.

Sunny   Just like me.

Ecstatic applause.

Mr. Destiny   It is up to us to write our stories. Up to us to build the roads we will walk down.

Unison (*chanting low, through end of scene*)   Wealth. Power. Fame. Honor. Wealth. Power. Fame. Honor.

Mr. Destiny   You control what happens. You create your beliefs. If you want to have been loved from your very first moment, believe that you were. Fight, Sunny. Reach out, grab your dreams by the balls and don't let go, until they become your reality. Go back to work. Talk to your boss. And CHANGE YOUR DESTINY!

Loud cheering. Techno music thunders through loudspeakers. Lights flash. Confetti falls from the sky. **Sunny** *and* **Ming-Ming** *dance triumphantly with unseen thousands.*

Seven

The countryside. **James** *is outside at sunrise. Muddy rubber boots are pulled over his city clothes. The sounds of birds, grasshoppers, cows, pigs, roosters and running water.* **Artemis** *enters.*

Artemis   That fucking rooster's been screeching since midnight.

James *smiles and opens his arms, breathing in the country air.*

James   Crickets sang outside my window. All night long. At dawn it was so foggy, when I held my hands in front of my face I couldn't see them. I should have woken you up.

Artemis   The documentary crew's been shooting this "hopelessly impoverished countryside" since sunrise. I'm sure I'll see footage.

James   I dreamed about us.

Artemis   Who was on top?

James   We were kids. Running through my father's fields, during rice harvest. Remember when we used to catch king grasshoppers, and bring them to your mother to roast?

Artemis   Nope.

James   It wasn't all bad.

Artemis   Not for the son of a farmer. Now − guess where we're having the premiere?

James   The Grand Hyatt?

Artemis   Too predictable. Think populist. Iconic. Stately.

James   The Summer Palace?

Artemis   Think giant bronze doors, facing the eastern skies. A banquet hall that feeds six thousand.

James   You didn't.

Artemis   McDonald's did it.

James   It's too much exposure.

Artemis   In every crisis there is opportunity.

James   She who opens her heart to ambition closes it to peace.

Artemis (*sarcastic*)   Let's have it at the country club. Afterwards we'll sip martinis, pat your poor little Chinese girls on the cheek, then squeeze in a round of golf.

James   The Great Hall of the People sends the wrong message.

Artemis   We're positioning your factory as an institution of social welfare that lifts peasants out of poverty. It's the perfect venue.

James   It's too high-profile.

Artemis   It's just a game, James. Play it − or cash in your chips.

James   It's not a game. This is our lives. You don't get to start over.

Artemis   Can't I be Buddhist and be reincarnated?

James   What will you be in your next life, a giant squid?

Artemis   And you can be the barnacles that cling to my tentacles.

James   It's too risky.

Artemis   When I say the word "Foxconn" – what comes to mind?

James *is silent.*

Artemis   Worker suicides. Reputation is everything. If you don't do this, you will lose control over your public image and Jade River will fall apart. Price-Smart is your biggest customer. If you want to maintain the life to which you've become accustomed, you have to do what they say.

James   What you say. *(Beat.)* The Great Hall of the People.

Artemis   And in it Jade River will rise from the ashes.

James   You still want a worker to intro the film?

Artemis   A cute, rosy-cheeked girl who is earnest, serious and stoic.

James   Like you were.

Artemis   I was never earnest.

James   I'll have my secretary organize an audition.

She kisses **James** *on the cheek.*

James   Stay for breakfast. The farmer's wife is making congee – with sweet potatoes. When was the last time you had a sweet potato?

Artemis   I don't eat them. They remind me of famine.

She exits.

Eight

Beijing International Airport. **Artemis** *emerges from the domestic terminal. She wears an elegant fall coat and pulls a sleek suitcase behind her. She's on the phone.*

Artemis *(into phone)*   That's fine. Read me the press list. *(She listens.)*

Qing Shu Min *approaches. She wears nondescript clothing, and smiles pleasantly.*

Qing Shu Min   Are you Artemis Chang?

Artemis *(back into phone)*   Add CNN, Al-Jazeera, *Nanjing Weekend, South China Morning Post* and the *Beijing Youth Daily*. Keep working on Central Television coverage.

Qing Shu Min   Are you Artemis Chang, Vice President of Price-Smart?

Artemis *puts away her phone.*

Artemis   Where's your sign?

Qing Shu Min   My sign?

Artemis   My driver should hold a sign with my name on it. So I can approach *her* when I'm ready.

Qing Shu Min   My apologies. Welcome to Beijing.

Artemis   Where are we parked?

Qing Shu Min   Right this way.

She takes **Artemis**'s *suitcase and leads her towards a parking garage.*

Artemis   It seems smoggier than usual.

Qing Shu Min   For a price, the weather bureau can seed the clouds to make it rain, so your event can happen on a blue sky day.

Artemis   That won't be necessary.

Qing Shu Min   I've been following your career for some time. It's nice to finally meet you. Not many women of your age have received such a prestigious education. Your parents must be very proud.

Artemis   What happened to the guy who usually gets me?

Qing Shu Min   His daughter has a piano recital.

Artemis   Where's the car?

Qing Shu Min   Just around the next corner.

Artemis   I need to go straight to Tiananmen.

Qing Shu Min   You don't want to freshen up at your hotel first?

Artemis   If I did I would request it.

Qing Shu Min   As you wish.

Artemis (*looking around*)   We're on the wrong floor.

Qing Shu Min   We are?

Artemis   There isn't a single vehicle in this section.

Qing Shu Min   How strange. I'm sure it's around here somewhere.

Artemis   Forget it. I'll call a cab.

She takes her suitcase and heads towards the terminal.

Qing Shu Min   It must be up one level. The numbers are very confusing.

Artemis   If you want to stay a driver get your shit together.

Qing Shu Min   A driver?

Artemis   Chauffer, transport technician, director of motor vehicle movement, whatever you people want to call it.

Qing Shu Min   I'm not any of those things.

Artemis   What?

Qing Shu Min   In the future, please be more careful about who you follow into dark corners.

Artemis *hesitates, looks around and starts to run towards the terminal.* **Gao Chen** *emerges from the shadows, thrusts a black hood over* **Artemis**'s *head, and tightens it. He drags her offstage, muffling her screams.* **Qing Shu Min** *follows, pulling* **Artemis**' *suitcase behind her.*

Nine

The banks of the Yangtze River, morning. **Li Han** *and* **Pete** *walk along the river. Each carries a pigeon-training basket in each hand. A cloth cover tied around each basket obscures the young pigeon within. They swing the baskets back and forth as they walk.*

Li Han   As soon as Taiwan and China are reunited we'll enter their races and win billions. Can you see it? A father-son team, training world-class racers.

Pete   I'd rather be poor and perform Monkey in teahouses –

Li Han (*interrupting*)   Yesterday in Taiwan a single pigeon was auctioned off for half a million. Imagine – one bird, worth more than a Mercedes. In the races last June no one knew she was special, then in the last six seconds of her seventh race she surged ahead –

Pete (*interrupting*)   My teacher told me about a school in Beijing where you learn the Monkey King –

Li Han (*interrupting*)   Tomorrow we'll start outdoor training.

Pete   Maybe, if I go to the factory and make money –

He follows too closely. His pigeon baskets crash into **Li Han**'s.

Li Han   Worthless shit!

Pete   I'm sorry –

Li Han   Sorry doesn't soothe their panic. Sorry doesn't mend a broken wing.

He sets down his baskets, then motions for **Pete** *to do the same.*

Pete   Is she hurt?

Li Han   Put them down!

Pete *sets the baskets down, more roughly than he should.* **Li Han** *pushes* **Pete** *to the ground.*

Pete   You said to swing the baskets.

Li Han   To give them air. To strengthen their wings. Not break them! They're young. They only know what we show them. If I released them and they had fear, they'd quake in their baskets and never go anywhere.

Pete   That's less idiotic than flying home.

Li Han   Racing birds defect all the time. Some guys lose their whole flock after one race. Do you know why mine return?

Pete   Because they're idiots.

Li Han   Rebellious birds don't become breeding stock. My line will yield champions. Spend more time in the loft. You'll inherit world-class racers.

Pete   I don't want world-class racers. I want to go to the factory. With Sunny –

Li Han   Your sister's a bad influence. It's time for her to come home.

Pete   You don't think she's a bad influence when you're spending her money.

Li Han *swings at* **Pete** *and misses. He coughs up blood.*

Pete   Ba –

Li Han   Go home.

Pete   Let me help you carry the –

Li Han (*interrupting*)   Go!

Pete *exits.* **Li Han** *wipes away the blood, checks the pigeons, then, carrying two baskets in each hand, continues along the path. He comes across* **Wang Hua**'s *pull-cart. From underneath comes the faint sound of a woman sobbing.*

Li Han   Auntie Wang? Is that you?

Wang Hua   Leave me alone.

Li Han   Are you drunk?

Wang Hua   Fuck off.

Li Han   What are you doing under there?

Wang Hua   I said go!

Li Han   Auntie Wang?

Wang Hua *crawls out from under the cart, greasy, bedraggled and bleary-eyed.*

Wang Hua   Huh?

She springs to her feet and pumps her fists towards the heavens.

(*Screaming.*) Bastard! Crook! Heartless son of a bitch! Give me back my son! Give him to me! My son! My son! My sonnn . . . He was so tall – so handsome. I should be dead. Not him! Not himmmm!

Li Han   Ran Feng's dead?

Wang Hua   You didn't tell him about Li Chen. You didn't talk him out of the strike. He was crushed by a bulldozer during the night.

Li Han   Auntie, I'm so sorry. What can I do?

Pete *enters, hanging back. Neither* **Li Han** *or* **Wang Hua** *see him.*

Wang Hua   It's too late. Those bastards cremated him before I could even take a last look at his beautiful face.

Li Han   Are they offering you a compensation package?

Wang Hua   The only package I want is my son, safe in my arms.

Li Han   Let Ran Feng care for you. How much are they offering?

Wang Hua   Eighty thousand, if I sign a waiver. Forty years of life, and that's what he's worth?

Li Han   Eighty thousand? That's more than he would have made in ten years.

Wang Hua   It's just paper. He's all alone now. No children. No wife. When I'm gone who will care for our afterlives?

A beat as **Li Han** *checks on his pigeons.*

Li Han   Forgive me, Auntie, but my daughter's not married, and your story is very heartbreaking.

Wang Hua   Ghost marriage? To a living woman?

Li Han   The wife of your son should care for you too.

Wang Hua   How much?

Li Han   Sign the waiver.

Wang Hua   Can she cook?

Li Han   Like the masters.

Wang Hua   What dishes?

She packs up her cart and starts to exit.

Li Han   You name it, she'll make it. Twice-cooked pork, stinky tofu, dan-dan noodles, steamed fish –

Wang Hua   Dan-dan noodles were Ran Feng's favorite.

Li Han   Sunny's are the best in the province.

Wang Hua   Sunny was two when Xiao Li passed. Who taught her?

Li Han   My mother.

Wang Hua   Liar. Your mother couldn't make ice cubes.

Li Han   Sunny will be home for New Year's. Don't take my word for it – come for dinner, you'll see that she's excellent daughter-in-law material!

He follows **Wang Hua** *off.* **Pete** *takes out his phone and makes a call.*

Ten

Factory bathroom, morning. Light streams through barred windows. **Sunny** *wears her factory uniform.* **Ming-Ming** *freshens* **Sunny***'s hair and excessive make-up. Both have new hairstyles.* **Sunny***'s phone rings. She silences it.*

Sunny *starts to speak.*

Ming-Ming   Look him straight in the eye.

Sunny *starts to speak.*

Ming-Ming   Don't use your high voice – it weakens your position.

Sunny *starts to speak.*

Ming-Ming   Don't smile right away – you'll seem too agreeable.

Sunny *(in a deep voice)*   "I've been a level-one sanitation technician for fifty months. I've done superior work and never failed an inspection."

Ming-Ming   Much better. If you stick with that delivery you will definitely get promoted.

Sunny   Thank you, Ming-Ming.

Ming-Ming   Thank yourself.

Sunny   No – really! If I hadn't met you, I wouldn't have taken the course, and I wouldn't have a diploma that says Harvard University!

Ming-Ming   You earned it, I earned my Oxford diploma, our brain circuits are rewired and our junk DNA is lit.

Sunny I should burn incense for the dead section manager –
if he hadn't jumped out the window there wouldn't be an open
management position.

Ming-Ming It's like Charles Darwin said – "Only the strong
survive."

Sunny You're strong. That's why you've lasted so long.

Ming-Ming In a year I'll be twenty-four and all my capital
will be used up. If I don't make it to an office position soon
they'll replace me with a fourteen-year-old with better eyes
and faster fingers.

Sunny They'd be idiots to do that. You have the best quality
control in your unit.

Ming-Ming This is your day. We'll work on my fate after
you get promoted. Take a deep breath. Find your center.

Sunny *closes her eyes, stands in prayer pose and centers with a deep*
"OM."

Ming-Ming You are beautiful.

Sunny I am beautiful.

Ming-Ming You are perfect.

Sunny I am perfect.

Ming-Ming You deserve this promotion.

Sunny I deserve to get promoted, live in the White House,
and be a princess.

Ming-Ming *hands* **Sunny** *a chunky, rhinestone-encrusted locket.*

Ming-Ming Keep this true image of success in your head.

Sunny *opens the locket, revealing a photo of* **Artemis Chang**.

Sunny It's perfect. Thank you.

She puts on the necklace.

Ming-Ming It's like Malcolm X said: "By Any Means
Necessary."

She exits. **Sunny** *assumes her Personal Power Position. Her phone rings. She turns it off.* **Old Lao** *enters with his clipboard and begins a routine quality inspection.* **Sunny** *reaches for the mop and cleans furiously.*

Old Lao   You lost your color. Your eyes are sunken. Are you sick?

Sunny   It's called make-up.

Old Lao   You look like a corpse of a whore given black eyes by her pimp.

Sunny   I appreciate your feedback. I'll evaluate this information and use it to improve my appearance so I can do a better job representing this factory and our glorious country.

Old Lao   Heheheh.

Sunny *(takes a deep breath, finds her center)*   Good morning.

Old Lao   Bad morning. There were worms in the congee.

Sunny   You should file a complaint.

Old Lao   Someone's getting ideas from a fancy petition.

Sunny   I'm not a political person. I'm just a person who deserves to be promoted to section manager.

Old Lao   Here we go again.

Sunny *(drops into her low voice)*   I've been a level-one sanitation technician for fifty months. I've done superior work and never failed a −

Old Lao *(interrupting)*   You are the most important person in the world. Your bowel movements are radiant. Full of meaning. If you wait for success you'll die in a sewer. Being a spoiled brat is the only worthwhile thing.

Sunny   I need a promotion.

Old Lao   I need to be hung like a donkey.

Sunny   Give me the job!

Old Lao   Give me a naked KTV waitress.

Sunny   Why are you so allergic to my success?

Old Lao   Why is every young person an idiot?

Sunny   Maybe we'd excel if we had more opportunities.

Old Lao   I gave you an opportunity three months ago.

Sunny   That wasn't an opportunity – that was a one-way ticket to jail.

Old Lao   So you read it!

Sunny   Don't change the subject.

Old Lao   Old Lao is slippery. Like a fish.

Sunny   Don't make me mad.

Old Lao   Oh no – you're so scary!

Sunny   Promote me.

Old Lao   No.

Sunny (*in her low voice*)   Promote me!

Old Lao   You young people are so brain-damaged.

Sunny   I deserve this opportunity for success.

Old Lao   I don't care what stupid sorrows you think you've lived through, compared to the past this is paradise. The Great Western Heaven.

Sunny   Last chance.

She takes a rubber cleaning glove off her right hand and advances towards **Old Lao**.

Old Lao   What are you going to do? Hit me?

Sunny   It's like Malcolm X said – "By Any Means Necessary."

She slips her hand into **Old Lao**'s *pants and gives him a hand job.*

Old Lao (*strangled*)   Huhhhhhh . . .

Sunny   Promote me.

Old Lao   Oh fuckkkk . . . fuck me fuuuuck meeee –

Sunny   Say it.

Old Lao   Oh God yes. Yesss . . .

Sunny   Say I'm promoted.

Old Lao   I'm promooooteddd –

Sunny   Tell me *I'm* promoted. "You're promoted, Sunny. You're promoted." Say it.

Old Lao   Shaddup shaddup don't get in the way of my huhhhhhh . . . . . .

Sunny   I'm the best. The most qualified. I deserve this position.

Old Lao   Huhh huhh huhh huhh huhhhh –

Sunny   "You're promoted." "You're promoted." Say it or I'll stop. Say it or I'll stop.

Old Lao   Don't stop – please please please don't stop ohh God dooooon't stoppppp . . .

Sunny *strokes him harder. Her phone rings again. The frenzied techno-pop love ballad plays over the next section.*

Sunny   Say it or I'll stop! I'm going to stop! I'm stopping –

Old Lao   You're promoted! You're promoted! You're – you're – Huhheehhheeeeuuiihhh-yuhhhhh-huhhhhhhhhhh!

He shudders and heaves into **Sunny***'s hands, knocking his glasses onto the floor.* **Sunny** *calmly removes her hand from his pants, wipes it on a towel, sprays it with a bleach solution, wipes it again, puts her glove back on, silences her phone and resumes cleaning the bathroom.*

Sunny   Thank you for this opportunity. I'll start tomorrow.

Old Lao *finds his glasses, puts them on, stares at* **Sunny***, then staggers off.* **Sunny** *contains herself until he exits, then repeats her Personal Power Position.*

End of Act One.

Intermission.

Act Two

One

Li Han's *rural home.* **Sunny** *enters, carrying the covered slop bucket. She wears an embroidered red qipao-style wedding dress. Her hair and make-up have been elaborately styled. She sets the slop bucket in its usual position.* **Pete** *enters and eyes the slop bucket.*

Sunny   Show me how a bride should stand.

Pete *shows* **Sunny** *a grand bridal stance. She tries it.*

Sunny   Like this?

Pete *arranges her body.*

Pete   Like this. And after you're married – like this.

He demonstrates how to walk like a just-married woman – with mincing steps and fluttering fingers.

Sunny   If you miss your cue and I get married by mistake I will wring your neck and turn you into soup.

Pete *eyes the slop bucket nervously.*

Sunny   Take out the petition.

Pete   Why?

Sunny   Do you want to give me a reading lesson or not?

Pete *pulls out a wadded up piece of paper and hands it to* **Sunny**.

Sunny *(reads, halting)*   We, the undersigned sanitation workers of Unit 27 are – *(To* **Pete**.*)* Dissatisfied?

Pete   Angry.

Sunny   Angry and – *(She pauses again, squinting at word.)*

Pete   Disgusted. Why did your unit manager give this to you?

Sunny *(shrugs, continues)*   We are tired of being treated unfairly. We demand the following changes.

Pete *glances at the door.*

Pete (*beat*)   Read the next section.

Sunny   We haven't gone over it.

Pete   They're easy characters.

Sunny (*reading*)   If you don't meet our –

Pete   Demands.

Sunny (*reading*)   We will go on a –

She looks at **Pete**, *but his eyes are on the door. He turns back to her.*

Pete   Strike.

Sunny   Idiots. (*Reading.*) We will go on a strike, and put a video on the –

Pete   Internet.

Sunny (*reading*)   That tells the whole . . . world about our –

Pete   Protest.

Sunny *crumbles the petition and throws it at* **Pete**. *He picks it up, smoothes out the pages and reads it.*

Sunny   Workers don't need a different life – just a new perspective.

Pete   What kind?

Sunny   The tragedy isn't that you don't have a Mercedes Benz. The tragedy is that you don't dare to long for one.

Pete   For what?

Sunny   A Mercedes! Don't forget – I used to be a bumpkin too. I didn't think I could change my life until I heard that sentence in a talk by the pioneer of success studies.

She readjusts the position of the slop bucket.

Pete   That's not where it was.

Sunny *moves it again.* **Pete** *puts it in the proper position.*

Sunny When I dared to want a Mercedes, I had the courage to change how I looked, spoke and behaved. Only then could I exploit my True Capital and get promoted to section manager.

Pete True Capital?

Sunny Youth is the True Capital of every migrant. You spend your youth in the factory, and in return for that investment receive skills and money. To exploit your own capital you must be your own master. You must be your own slave. Only then will your destiny change.

Pete You're still a janitor.

Sunny I'm a sanitation technician. It's temporary. Soon I'll get an office position and rely on my brains instead of my body.

Li Han *and* **Wang Hua** *enter.* **Li Han** *carries a foldable altar table.* **Wang Hua**, *who is dressed in gaudy rural fashion, carries a framed photo of* **Ran Feng** *and an urn full of his ashes. They create a makeshift altar in the center of the room, and decorate it with a string of blinking lights.* **Sunny** *places a platter of breaded, deep-fried meat on the altar, lights a stick of incense, then approaches* **Wang Hua**.

Wang Hua To avoid paying a marriage tax, we'll marry you in the old style. The bride and groom will face each other and say "I marry you" three times.

Sunny Ran Feng's dead. How will he speak?

Wang Hua I'm his mother. I will say his words for him.

Sunny Goodbye, Ba. After this I won't be your daughter.

Li Han Work hard. Listen to Auntie. Make sure she gets good value for her money.

Wang Hua *pulls a "red envelope" out of her purse and gives it to* **Li Han**. *He pockets it.*

Li Han Thank you Auntie. I'm glad we can now be one family.

Wang Hua (*to* **Sunny**) Face your husband.

Sunny (*motioning toward meat*)   Ba promised I could cook. Quality inspection's important.

Wang Hua   Wait till the incense is burnt. Ran Feng should try it first.

Li Han *takes a piece and bites into it.*

Li Han   Go ahead, Auntie. Sneak preview.

Wang Hua *takes a spicy wing and eats it.* **Sunny** *has one too.*

Li Han   Pete. Celebrate your sister.

Pete   I'm not hungry.

Wang Hua   You pass Quality Inspection. Now –

Wang Hua *takes the framed portrait of* **Ran Feng** *off the altar and holds it in front of her face.*

Wang Hua   Face your husband.

Sunny *faces the portrait of* **Ran Feng**.

Wang Hua   Sunny Li, this is Ran Feng speaking. Take good care of my mother. Cook her fresh congee each morning, beef noodles for lunch, and fish and vegetables for supper. Clip her nails, rub her feet, pick wax out of her ears and when she is too old to trim her nose hairs, do it for her. If you fail to perform these duties I will haunt you in this life and beat you in the next. I marry you. I marry you. I marry you.

Sunny *makes eye-contact with* **Pete**.

Wang Hua   He's done. Say your part.

Pete *tosses a single pigeon feather on the floor. No one but* **Sunny** *sees him do it.*

Sunny   What's that?

She picks the feather off the floor and examines it.

Wang Hua   Finish your wedding.

Sunny   I marry you. I marry you. I –

Pete *tosses a handful of pigeon feathers onto the floor. Only* **Sunny** *sees them. She picks up the feathers.*

Sunny (*to* **Ran Feng**)   What are you trying to say?

Wang Hua   He's saying finish the marriage, slow-poke, my mother's getting angry!

Sunny   Maybe he's saying he doesn't want to marry me.

Wang Hua   Sunny Li, this is Ran Feng. Speaking. Again. Finish marrying me at once. Then we will retire to the bridal chamber my mother prepared and my spirit can finally rest!

Sunny   But Ran Feng, you keep sending me feathers. Maybe you want pigeons in the afterlife, not me.

Li Han *examines the feathers, then heads to the loft.*

Wang Hua   Can a pigeon clean my mother's ears? Can it cook her crispy eggplant?

Li Han *storms in.*

Li Han   What is this? What is the meaning of this?

Wang Hua   Finish the ceremony.

Li Han (*to* **Sunny**)   Where are my birds? Where are my babies? Where did they go? Tell me – tell me!

Sunny   I don't know. Maybe they went where all babies go. Correction. Not all babies. Just the ones you don't want.

A long silence. **Li Han** *approaches the closed slop bucket. He slowly lifts the lid – then lets out a silent, grief-stricken scream. He reaches in, pulls out a giant mound of pigeon feathers, and sinks to his knees, cradling the massive armload of feathers like a baby.* **Pete** *makes eye-contact with* **Sunny**, *then exits.*

Li Han (*to feathers*)   My heart. My darlings.

Wang Hua   Idiot girl. Look what you've done to your father. Those birds belonged to his brother.

Sunny   Did not. Ba doesn't have a brother.

Wang Hua   You know nothing.

Li Han (*to feathers*)   I'm sorry.

Sunny   You never asked me the name of my dish.

Li Han (*to feathers*)   I'm so sorry.

Sunny   It's called "Pigeons Coming Home to Roost."

Li Han *stares at the feathers, and convulses. Trying to keep it all in.*

Sunny   Dark meat. Fatty skin. That's why it's so succulent.

She places the platter of meat in front of **Li Han**.

Sunny   Get it while it's fresh. We really shouldn't waste it.

Pete *enters and hands* **Sunny** *a giant denim backpack.* **Sunny** *puts it on and exits.* **Pete** *follows her out.* **Wang Hua** *reaches into* **Li Han***'s pocket, retrieves her "red envelope" full of money. She sets the string of blinking lights on the ground, collapses the altar table, then exits with the table, framed photo of* **Ran Feng** *and urn.* **Li Han** *remains on the floor, beside a string of blinking lights, his arms full of feathers.*

Two

Night on the banks of the Yangtze River. **Sunny** *enters, accompanied by* **Pete**. *Each carries one side of a large denim duffel bag.* **Sunny** *is still wearing the silk wedding dress.*

Pete   We got off at the wrong stop.

Sunny   Old people were crushing me! If we'd stayed on another minute I would have fainted.

Pete   Next time elbow them.

Sunny   That wouldn't have helped. We were at the front of the line and they pushed past us, like it was the last bus on earth. Someone should write a self-help book that teaches old people how to be civilized.

Pete They're old. Maybe they remember a time when there wouldn't be another bus.

Sunny It's not that time now. They need to change their perspective and dare to be braver.

Pete I'm tired. My shoulder hurts.

Sunny Fine. Rest.

They set down the bag.

If you worked in the garden you'd be stronger.

Pete I'm not going back.

Sunny You're almost finished with high school.

Pete I'm not learning anything. All my friends have left for the city. It's just me and a bunch of babies.

Sunny Just two more years. You have to finish.

Pete Two more years invested in stupidity is two years of capital wasted. I'm dying here. I'm surrounded by ugly farms and stupid people. It's my destiny to work in the city. Then I can save up for opera school and realize my dreams.

Sunny I have one train ticket and no money. Even if I had money I couldn't take you – tickets have been sold out for weeks.

Pete Nothing's impossible if you believe in your heart you can succeed.

Sunny Don't quote my inspirational sayings back to me.

Pete *opens one of* **Sunny**'s *duffel bags and dumps out the contents, strewing clothes, blankets, Pringle canisters and Snickers bars on the ground.*

Sunny Fucking rice bucket! What the hell are you doing?

Pete Believing.

He steps into the duffel bag, curls up tight, then tucks his head in. He barely fits.

Sunny   It's thirty hours to Shenzhen. You can't stay in there for that long.

Pete   I need money so I can go to opera school. My life is wasted here. It is my destiny to perform Monkey King.

Sunny   Suck in your stomach.

Pete   I'm not fat.

Sunny   I will leave a blanket on the banks of this river, but I'm not going to Shenzhen without my snacks.

She pushes her food back into the bag.

Pete   Ow! You're scraping me!

Sunny   You should have thought about that before changing your destiny.

*She shoves **Pete**'s head into the bag, and zips it up.*

Sunny   Can you breathe?

Pete   Barely.

Sunny   What's that sound?

Pete *(muffled)*   What sound?

Sunny *unzips the bag and finds **Pete**'s mouth is crammed full of Pringles.*

Sunny   My chips!

Pete *(mouth full)*   Barbecue. My favorite.

Sunny   Walk to the train station, then get in my bag. Eat more of my snacks, and I'll dump you on the tracks.

Pete *gets out of the bag and bows profusely, still chewing his chips.*

Pete *(mouth full)*   Thank you. You won't regret this. Thank you. Thank you!

Sunny   In the city, everything moves really fast. You won't have time to think. Everything that gets in the way of being a worker, leave on the banks of this river. Nobody cares that you're the only son, or the hope of seven generations. All that

matters are the movements you make with your body. You'll
sink or swim on that ability.

Pete   I can be a good worker.

Sunny   Then you have to change, and leave your lazy ways
behind.

Pete *cups his hands, casting a spell.*

Pete (*into his cupped hands*)   I choose the trick of the Earthly
Conclusion! Seventy-Two Transformations!

Sunny   Close your eyes.

Pete *complies.*

Sunny   Imagine everything you don't need flying out of your
fingers and toes, back into the dirt and sky. Empty your mind.
Become a machine. When you open your eyes, you will be a
new person. Your life will be wide open with possibility. It will
be beautiful and blank. Things will be hard. You will get tired.
But if you believe in yourself, you can do anything. Do you
believe in yourself, Pete?

Pete   Yes. I believe.

Sunny   Then hold out your arms, like you're flying.

They do this together.

Let the countryside fade away. Let go of your past. Face your
future with clear eyes, and a strong body. Are you ready?

Pete   I'm ready.

Sunny   Then take a deep breath. (*They do this together.*) Now,
change.

They open their eyes and gaze forward.

Three

An interrogation room at a Beijing police station. **Artemis** *sits at a table.*
Gao Chen *sits across from her.* **Qing Shu Min** *enters. She carries a*

*tray containing a metal teapot, plastic cups, and a bowl of roasted
watermelon seeds. She pours three cups of tea, removes* **Artemis***'s hood
and smiles.*

Qing Shu Min   Did you have a nice nap?

Artemis *looks around, disoriented.*

Qing Shu Min   Don't worry. You are as safe as you want
to be.

Artemis   Bring me your supervisor.

Qing Shu Min   Have some tea.

Artemis   We could have settled this at the airport. How
much do you want?

Gao Chen *approaches* **Artemis**. *He hovers over her.*

Qing Shu Min   It's not polite to refuse what your host offers.
Didn't they teach that at Harvard?

Artemis *sips the tea.* **Gao Chen** *takes the bowl of roasted
watermelon seeds and returns to his seat. He cracks a seed open with his
teeth, eats the inside, and tosses the shell onto the table. He does this for
the rest of the scene.*

Artemis   There's cash in my purse. If you get it we can
settle this.

Qing Shu Min   Unfortunately, not everyone's for sale. Some
people have values they refuse to abandon.

Artemis   What's this about?

Qing Shu Min   Your past. Catching up with you.

Artemis   I haven't broken any laws. Personally or with my
company.

Qing Shu Min   Ah, but in China you aren't just you. You
are your family, too.

She drops a folder on the table. **Artemis** *opens it and finds a collection
of black-and-white photographs.*

Qing Shu Min   Let the past be a fleeting storm cloud, forgotten once the sun emerges. Why waste strength carrying umbrellas on blue-sky days? Or do you cling to the memory of the storm, afraid you might not know who you are without it? Do you want it to rain, Ms. Chang?

Artemis (*staring at pictures*)   What is this?

Qing Shu Min   You don't recognize them? (*Clicks tongue in disapproval.*)

Artemis   I know who they are. What I don't know is why I'm drinking bad tea in a police station, looking at their pictures.

Qing Shu Min   If the tea is weak we can make another pot.

Gao Chen *rises.*

Artemis   Don't trouble yourself.

Gao Chen *sits and resumes eating watermelon seeds.*

Qing Shu Min   This tea was a gift from the *Governor* of Taiwan. Take smaller sips and swish it through your mouth before swallowing. Be patient. Give your taste buds a chance to receive the full flavor.

Artemis *takes another sip of tea.*

Qing Shu Min   Now, please. Identify the people in the picture.

Artemis   This is my uncle and aunt on their wedding day. This is my grandfather, holding me after my naming ceremony. (*Beat.*) These are my parents.

Qing Shu Min   Where are your relatives now?

Artemis   They're dead.

Qing Shu Min   All of them?

Artemis   I don't know what happened to my mother.

Qing Shu Min   But the rest?

Artemis   The rest were executed.

Qing Shu Min   You had a secret room in your house where your grandfather hid his books. A neighbor found out and reported your family to the village committee.

Artemis   Correct.

Qing Shu Min   You were never punished.

Artemis   I was six.

Qing Shu Min   But now you're an adult, and know better.

Artemis   How old are you?

Qing Shu Min   Twenty-seven.

Artemis   If the past is a fleeting storm cloud you haven't felt a drop of rain in your life.

Qing Shu Min *pulls a large photo out of an envelope and places it face down in front of* **Artemis**. **Artemis** *starts to turn it over.* **Qing Shu Min** *stops her.*

Qing Shu Min   How many of your girlhood wishes, the things you longed for, turned out to be what you wanted when you finally got them?

Artemis   My girlhood wishes?

Qing Shu Min   When you look back on your path to this moment, was it worth it? Or did you build a nightmare, then find yourself stuck living it?

Artemis   The past was the nightmare.

Qing Shu Min   Yes, and it's over. But perhaps you never woke up, opened the window and realized everything's okay. Maybe you're lazy, and keep your eyes shut even though everyone else is awake.

Artemis   Why am I here?

Qing Shu Min   How about we trade intelligence?

Artemis   About?

Qing Shu Min   Your business venture.

Artemis   I have many.

Qing Shu Min   The one that resulted in the daughter of counter-revolutionaries staging an event inside the Great Hall of the People.

Artemis   This is about the premiere?

Qing Shu Min   Subversives are sent to asylums for the politically insane. They are medicated and given electric treatments until their condition is stabilized.

Artemis   I'm not a subversive.

Qing Shu Min   Then what are you?

Artemis   A glorified publicist. That's it.

Qing Shu Min   You are conducting a high profile event in a symbolic building located on the most politically sensitive public space in the nation.

Artemis   It's a PR stunt, designed to improve the corporate image of my company and our largest supplier.

Qing Shu Min   You have no political intentions?

Artemis   I'm a vice president in a multinational corporation. All I care about is money.

Qing Shu Min   I hope I don't need to explain the importance of maintaining stability and social harmony so that we can pursue economic success and improve our gross domestic happiness.

Artemis   You could improve that appearance and how the world sees you by choosing less violent tactics.

Qing Shu Min   Why would we change when everyone wants to sleep with us just the way we are?

Artemis   If you were comfortable with your PR image I wouldn't be here.

Qing Shu Min   These are sensitive times. Not a time for protest, proclamation or any kind of dissent. Understand?

Artemis   Of course.

Qing Shu Min   Here's my card. (*Hands it to her.*) Notify me immediately if you come across anything suspicious.

Qing Shu Min *takes the folder of photos. She leaves one in front of* **Artemis**.

Artemis   Is there something else you would like me to look at?

Qing Shu Min   If you wish.

Artemis   If I wish?

Qing Shu Min   It's your mother.

Artemis   My mother?

Qing Shu Min   Yes. At the moment of her death.

Gao Chen *and* **Qing Shu Min** *exit.* **Artemis** *puts on her coat, takes her suitcase and starts to exit. She pauses, takes the photograph and exits, without looking at it.*

Four

Factory office, waiting room. **Sunny**, *dressed in her factory uniform, sits in a row of metal folding chairs.* **Ming-Ming** *enters, dressed in office clothing, wearing a lot of make-up and jewelry.*

Sunny   Ming-Ming!

Ming-Ming   Sunny!

Sunny   I almost didn't recognize you.

Ming-Ming   I'm here for the audition.

Sunny   Me too!

Ming-Ming   You're auditioning?

Sunny   Of course! Were we supposed to dress up?

Ming-Ming (*beat*)   If you look like the people you want to become, your chances of being accepted will improve by sixty-nine percent.

Sunny   I look stupid. I should change.

Ming-Ming   Don't worry about it. Just be yourself.

Sunny   What have you gone over?

Ming-Ming   The things I'm learning in night school.

Sunny   You're re-taking the course?

Ming-Ming   That was just level one self-improvement. You can never stop learning and improving yourself. The minute you do, you give up.

Sunny   What are you studying now?

Ming-Ming   Public Speaking. Centering Methods. Theories of Eye Contact . . . and Smile Dynamics.

Sunny   Smile Dynamics?

Ming-Ming   There's an optimal number of seconds to wait before smiling, depending on the status of the recipient.

Sunny   How many seconds should I wait with these bosses?

Ming-Ming   It's too late to think about that. Whatever I say will confuse you.

Sunny   What about eye-contact?

Ming-Ming   You took the level-one class. Go over what they taught you.

Sunny   There wasn't anything on Eye-Contact Theory!

Ming-Ming   You established Eye-Contact with your unit manager in order to get the promotion, didn't you?

Sunny (*lowers voice*)   The things they taught us in class didn't cover my situation. I used other methods.

Ming-Ming   Other methods? What do you mean?

Sunny *whispers into* **Ming-Ming**'s *ear.*

Ming-Ming　That wasn't in the class. Who taught you that strategy?

Sunny　I . . . read a book.

Ming-Ming　What book?

Sunny　Advanced . . . Negotiation Tactics.

Ming-Ming　Show me the technique. Step by step.

Sunny　There's not enough time. Whatever I say will confuse you.

Ming-Ming　I thought you were a person worthy of investment.

Sunny　In what? Friendship?

Ming-Ming　Level-Two Self-Improvement goes into deep detail about the importance of investing in a Social Network for Upward Mobility. It's a ladder. Of relationships. You climb to succeed. Only one worker will represent the factory in Beijing. I've spent ten years training for this moment. I know exactly what to do.

Sunny　It's like you said – I'm younger than you. I have capital left. This is *your* last chance. Don't waste it.

Ming-Ming　Fuck your ancestors.

James *enters.*

James　Hello, ladies. I'm afraid Ms. Chang –

Artemis *strides in, looking more poised than ever.*

Artemis (*to girls*)　Stand up please. Look left. Look right. Look at me. Smile.

They follow her directions.

Artemis　Repeat after me "Ladies and gentlemen, welcome to the Great Hall of the People."

Sunny/Ming-Ming (*stumbling over each other*)   Ladies and gentlemen, welcome –

Artemis (*to* **Ming-Ming**)   You first.

Ming-Ming (*like airline hostess*)   Ladies and gentlemen, welcome to the Great Hall of the People.

Sunny (*like cheerleader*)   Ladies and gentlemen, welcome to the Great Hall of the People!

Artemis (*to girls*)   Thank you. That's all.

James *and* **Artemis** *start to exit.* **Sunny** *approaches them.*

Sunny (*earnest, simple*)   Ladies and gentlemen, welcome to the Great Hall of the People.

Ming-Ming (*copying* **Sunny**'*s tone*)   Ladies and gentlemen, welcome to the Great Hall of the People.

James *and* **Artemis** *turn around.*

Artemis   Relax. Act natural.

Sunny   It's such an honor to stand before you magnificent, kind people –

Ming-Ming   and share my humble story.

Sunny   Working at Jade River Manufacturing has made my life a success –

Ming-Ming   If it wasn't for the management's generous spirit and benevolent behavior, I wouldn't have been able to –

Sunny/Ming-Ming (*in unison*)   Change My Destiny.

James *pulls out his phone, takes a photo of them and examines it. He points to the screen.* **Ming-Ming** *subtly imitates* **Artemis**' *body language.*

James   Too Western.

Artemis   The message should be "grateful peasant."

Ming-Ming   Hello, madam. My name is Ming-Ming Chen. Please allow me to share my résumé, which highlights my qualifications.

Artemis   That won't be necessary.

Ming-Ming   Please, kind lady, allow me to point out the number of years I've worked, which illustrates my commitment –

Artemis *(interrupting)*   We've made our decision.

Ming-Ming *turns to* **James**.

Ming-Ming   Nice to meet you, sir. My name is Ming-Ming Chen and I am the worker with the right qualifications.

James   We've made our decision.

Ming-Ming *lunges towards* **James***' crotch in an attempt to give him a hand-job. He pushes her away. She stumbles and falls to the floor.*

Ming-Ming   It is my destiny to make lots of money.

Artemis   Leave before I call security.

Ming-Ming *(about* **Sunny***)*   She's an idiot. The only reason she's here is because I took pity on her. I have experience – I'm the best worker.

Artemis   You're fired.

Ming-Ming *(to* **Sunny***)*   I taught you how to behave. I lit your junk DNA.

Sunny   You heard the bosses.

Ming-Ming   I'm too old. I don't have enough capital to start over.

Artemis   Go.

Ming-Ming   If I leave I'll have to go back to the countryside, marry an idiot farmer and spend my life making children.

Sunny   Go.

Ming-Ming *exits.* **Artemis** *hands* **Sunny** *a typed-out sheet of paper, written in Chinese characters.*

Artemis   Here's your speech. Memorize it. You'll deliver it in Beijing in June. Do a good job and we'll promote you to a nice front office position.

Sunny *opens the locket she's wearing and shows the image to* **Artemis.**

Sunny   To achieve your goals you need to keep a true image of success in your head.

Artemis   I'm your image of success?

Sunny   Thanks to you my dreams are coming true.

Artemis   Maybe it's time for better dreams. Leave your contact information with the secretary. She'll arrange our next meeting.

Sunny *shakes* **Artemis** *and* **James**' *hands and exits.*

Artemis   I need a drink.

James   You were missing for two weeks.

Artemis   Not answering your calls doesn't make me lost.

James   I know where you were.

Artemis   Then I wasn't missing.

James   I tried to warn you –

Artemis   This is my fault?

James   What did they do to you?

Artemis   It was very civilized. They served me tea. And roasted watermelon seeds.

James   Sorrow shared divides.

Artemis   Bullshit. Sorrow shared makes everyone infected. Smart people keep their distance and avoid contamination.

James   I've known you for fifty years. Whatever you have – I've caught it.

Artemis *takes a black-and-white photograph out of her purse and hands it to* **James**.

Artemis   A young woman with a long black braid kneels in front of a fence. She's wearing a white shirt and dark pants. Her eyes are open. Her face is calm. She's flying and falling all at once. What do you suppose she's thinking, as that bullet's exiting her head?

James   Maybe she's thinking about you.

Artemis   Remember when I wanted to be a teacher?

James   Like your mother.

Artemis   Or an intellectual, like my grandfather. But then – then I wanted to be very rich.

James   So you could take care of yourself.

Artemis   If they'd lived there'd be pressure to have children. Trips home to read classics to my father and cook fish for my mother. I would have caved in, gotten married, and wondered what I might have done if I wasn't living under some man's thumb.

James   You're free.

Artemis   To close my eyes, make money and spend it on pretty things.

James   You have other options.

Artemis   There are only two roads to walk down. There were only ever two choices. You can see the truth – and always be in pain. Or we can look away and be rich. And safe. And happy.

James   Classic Artemis. Reducing life on earth to a binary. Truth or happiness. Wealth or understanding.

Artemis   Excuse me?

James   Ever since we left the countryside you have seen everything as something to conquer. So you can prove – to who, I don't know – that you are worth something. When was the last time you felt joy? I mean real ecstasy, not just the thrill of the hunt?

Artemis   Fuck you.

James   Do you even know how to not be in control? Can you ever just be a feather, floating in the wind?

Artemis   That feather belonged to a chicken that is dead because it isn't a hawk.

James   You're not a hawk or a chicken. You're not really even Artemis. Your name is Chang Li Hua and I loved you. Just the way you were.

A long, complicated silence, as **Artemis** *looks at* **James**. *It's unclear whether she's going to collapse into his arms or slap him. Finally she retrieves the photograph of her mother, puts it in her purse, and exits.*

Five

Factory bathroom. **Pete** *mops the floor. A janitor's cart is nearby.* **Sunny** *saunters in.* **Pete** *ignores her.*

Sunny   Something's different about me. Something's changed. Can you see it?

Pete   You look the same. You always look the same.

Sunny   It's too soon to tell. Tomorrow you'll notice.

Pete   Just say it.

Sunny   I won the audition! I'm going to Beijing!

Pete   To talk to stuck-up city people.

Sunny   Before, my future was a food stall in a dusty alley, that sold steamed buns to a few customers. Now it's McDonald's – Clean. Bright. Highly efficient.

Pete   Who's writing your speech?

Sunny   It will be my face on television, representing the workers. My mouth, saying the words. Help me with some characters. I'll say your name on TV as special thanks.

Pete   I'm busy.

Sunny   How about after your shift?

Pete   How about you read this?

Pete *pulls the petition out of his pocket and holds it out to* **Sunny**, *who snatches it and shoves it into her pocket.*

Sunny   That's an illegal petition!

Pete   You said you want to represent the workers. You already know all the characters.

Sunny   They'd lock me up forever and send you the bill.

Pete   The countryside was fine.

Sunny   You hated it.

Pete   You made me hate it. I had time there. People looked at my face when I passed them.

Sunny *cups her hands in front of her, as if she's holding something precious inside them.* **Ming-Ming** *enters from a shower stall, wearing a robe over her clothes. She is in a dissociative state.* **Sunny** *and* **Pete** *don't notice her, and continue speaking.*

Ming-Ming (*to herself, softly*)   Excellence is a habit. We are what we do. One who feels failure limits her activities. Success is dependent on effort.

Sunny (*sarcastic*)   You have two methods of escape. Which would you like to learn?

Pete   I know what your problem is. I've finally figured it out.

Sunny   Your first choice is the Trick of the Male Heir.

Pete   You think you're the only person who has dreams and wants things.

Sunny   Go home. Mine coal. Make sons.

Ming-Ming *approaches* **Sunny**, *but sees someone else.*

Ming-Ming (*dazed*)   Hello, madam. My name is Ming-Ming Chen. It is such a pleasure to meet you.

Sunny   Ming-Ming. It's Sunny. You know me.

Ming-Ming (*to* **Pete**)   Good day, sir. It's an honor to make your acquaintance.

She offers **Pete** *her hand. He shakes it and finds his hand covered in blood. He shows* **Sunny** *the blood.* **Sunny** *pushes up the sleeves of* **Ming-Ming**'*s robe and finds long cuts along her arms.*

Ming-Ming (*still detached*)   Louder. Dig deeper. You die in a field if you fail to commit.

Sunny   Get help.

Pete *exits.* **Ming-Ming** *assumes her Personal Power Position.* **Sunny** *tries to make her comfortable.*

Ming-Ming   I am the most important person in the world. The things I say and do are important

Sunny/Ming-Ming   They are full of meaning. If I wait for success I will fail. Action is the only worthwhile thing. I am the most important person in the world. The things I say and do are important. They are full of meaning. If I wait for success I will fail. Action is the only worthwhile thing.

Old Lao *enters with a first-aid kit.* **Pete** *follows him in.*

Old Lao   The only thing worse than a factory worker killing herself is one who can't finish the job.

Sunny   She's bleeding. We have to bandage her cuts.

Old Lao   So she can try it again in a week? No. Even the hell she'll go to will be better than what we lived through in the fifties.

Sunny (*to* **Ming-Ming**)   Keep your arms above your heart.

She tries to wrench the first-aid kit from **Old Lao**. *He resists.*

Old Lao   I've watched you kids moan through this factory for decades. None of you eat bitterness. None of you know pain.

Sunny   You don't know us.

Old Lao *pushes* **Sunny** *away. She returns to* **Ming-Ming**'s *side.*

Old Lao   You don't know how quiet it gets when there's no animals around. No insects because all the plants are dead. No children crying because they don't have the energy. Do you know what I'm talking about? Are you listening?!

Sunny   If you want me to listen – help!

Old Lao *takes over* **Ming-Ming**'s *first aid.*

Old Lao   In the fifties and sixties Mao wanted to become the most prosperous nation – by exploiting his "greatest natural resource."

Sunny   Coal.

Old Lao   Peasants. (*To* **Ming-Ming**.) You're fine. You didn't cut deep enough. We took apart our houses and melted down our tools. We gave away our clothes, lived in communes, and carried the nation to prosperity. On our backs. "By Any Means Necessary."

Sunny   Did it work?

Old Lao   Shut up! Clean mess.

Sunny *mops the floor.* **Pete** *hangs back and listens quietly.*

Old Lao   To increase grain production, Mao made us kill all the sparrows. He thought they were eating the grain.

Pete   Sparrows don't eat grain.

Old Lao   They eat the locusts that eat the grain. By the time Mao changed his policy – it was too late. All the crops were gone. Local officials staged photos to prove how full and happy we were.

Sunny (*bitchy*)   Why didn't *you* starve?

Old Lao   I had a little brother. Pang-Pang. One minute he
was beside me. Too hungry to move. Then my mother carried
him to our neighbor. We got their youngest son in return. I
watched my father's hands shake as he held a curtain over that
little boy's head. So the gods couldn't see us. My mother slit his
throat. I caught his blood in a bucket. I made soup. So nothing
would be wasted.

Sunny *starts to speak.*

Old Lao (*cutting her off*)   Hitler killed eleven million and the
world still feels bad. Mao killed five times that many − of his
own people − and what do foreigners want when they come to
China? His little red book, and a shirt with his face on it. If
you kids want to kill yourselves be my guest − but do it because
you understand what has happened. Not because you missed
some made-up opportunity for success.

Old Lao *exits.* **Sunny** *and* **Pete** *help* **Ming-Ming** *stand and walk
towards the door.*

Ming-Ming   Last week, after Mr. Destiny got in a cab, I got
in another and followed him home.

Sunny   Shhh. You had a big shock. Conserve your energy.

Ming-Ming   I wanted to see what his mansion looked like,
so I'd have a true image of success in my head.

Sunny   Don't think about that now.

Ming-Ming   Mr. Destiny lives in a shack lined with cardboard
and plastic bags. It's not even his own shack − he shares it. It's
worse than our dorms.

Sunny   Maybe he was visiting someone.

Ming-Ming   He's a peasant. Like us. He just wears a
different uniform.

Sunny   Rest at home. Come back to the city when you feel
stronger.

Ming-Ming   Don't worry. Next time I'll commit. I'll succeed. Satisfaction guaranteed.

Ming-Ming *exits.* **Pete** *glares at* **Sunny,** *then exits.* **Sunny** *remains. She mops the floor.*

Six

A video-game arcade in Shenzhen. **Pete,** *dressed in street clothes, plays a shoot-'em-up game in two-player mode. He has a gun in each hand and is completely engrossed.* **Sunny** *enters, also in street clothes.* **Pete** *ignores her.*

Sunny   I've been trying to call you for two weeks.

Pete   . . .

Sunny   I went to your dorm. Your roommate said you'd moved out.

Pete   . . .

Sunny   I'm going to Beijing tomorrow. Wish me luck.

Pete   . . .

Sunny *wrenches one of the guns out of* **Pete***'s hands and plays alongside him.*

Sunny   Get the energy pack.

Pete   Get your own energy pack.

Sunny   I have full strength.

Pete *shoots* **Sunny***'s avatar.*

Sunny   Pete!

Pete   Get the energy pack.

Sunny   Why did you leave?

Pete   Behind you.

They focus on shooting zombies.

Pete   Reload.

Sunny   I'm out of ammo –

Pete   Take the pack.

Sunny   I memorized my speech.

Pete   Get that guy –

Sunny   That's a girl, I'll lose points –

Pete   She's a zombie – GET HER!

Sunny   Are you sure?

Pete *tries to grab his second gun back from* **Sunny**. *He is unsuccessful.*

Pete   I'm fine on my own. I don't need your stupid help – it's not help. It's just bad advice. And poison.

Sunny   Shut your fucking face. You're distracting me.

They focus on the game.

Pete   City people play a computer game where they pretend to be farmers. They plant seeds, harvest vegetables and get points for stealing crops.

Sunny   You made that up.

Pete   A doctor messed up a heart surgery because he'd stayed up guarding his computer vegetables and didn't get enough sleep.

Sunny   Why do they want to be farmers?

Zombie attack from all sides. The game gets intense, fast and furious.
Sunny *and* **Pete** *go into shoot-'em-up overdrive.*

Pete   They're fake farmers. Growing vegetables they can't even eat.

Sunny   They're crazy.

Pete   You want to be a fake city person.

Sunny   The Monkey King wasn't fake just because he had lots of transformations.

Pete   His transformations were temporary, idiot. As soon as the danger was gone he turned back into himself. Even when Monkey turned into a rock, the rock had a monkey's tail. You always knew it was him. Reload.

Sunny   Monkey never loses his tail? I don't remember that part of the story –

Pete   Reload!

Sunny   I could spend the rest of my life here but unless I marry a city person I'll live and die with no rights and nothing that a city person is guaranteed from the moment they are born until their last breath on earth. If I had kids I'd have to pay half my salary every month for tuition even though the same school's free if you're from the city.

Pete   Use the flame-thrower.

Sunny   Where do you sleep?

Pete   Train station.

Sunny   Why did you leave the factory?

Pete   I was riding the bus. A group of city kids got on and tried to make me give up my seat. None of the other peasants were in seats. They were squatting on the floor.

Sunny   What did they do?

Pete *focuses on playing the game.*

Pete   When I got off at my stop they followed me.

Sunny   To the factory?

Pete   They dragged me to an alley and threw me into a pile of bricks.

Sunny   . . .

Pete   They kicked me until I was covered in dirt, then stopped and said I was too filthy to touch their shoes.

They play the game.

Before they left, they took turns pissing on me.

They play the game.

Know why I like the train station?

Sunny Why?

Pete It's full of peasants who act like peasants.

Sunny Let's go to the police. We can file a report –

Pete *lowers the gun.*

Pete They ate our brains.

Sunny What?

Pete *(motioning to screen)* Game over.

He starts to exit, limping.

Sunny Wish me luck on my speech.

Pete *(angry)* What's the point of surviving pig slop if you're going to be a zombie?

He exits.

Sunny *(calling after him)* I can't live in the countryside. I can't be a city person. How else can I act? Who should I be?

Seven

Countryside. Banks of the Yangtze River. **Sunny** *enters carrying her overstuffed backpack. She approaches* **Wang Hua,** *who sits by her pull-cart polishing a pair of leather boots.*

Sunny Auntie Wang.

Wang Hua Sorry. I'm closed.

Sunny It's Sunny.

Wang Hua You're too late. My business went elsewhere. You're not the only girl who can rub feet and pick ears.

Sunny   I'm on my way to Beijing. I walked by my house. I had to see it. It's the only place that never changes.

Wang Hua *hands* **Sunny** *a boot and rag.* **Sunny** *polishes it.*

Sunny   You're the only person who's known me my whole life. Besides Ba . . . and Pete. Even though you tried to murder me.

Wang Hua   Don't take that slop bucket thing personally. I fixed a hundred girls before you and another fifty after. You were no different.

Sunny   I'm alive. That's different.

Wang Hua *takes the boot back from* **Sunny**, *inspects her shoeshine job, hacks a loogie on the boot and hands it back for more polishing.*

Sunny   I need your help.

Wang Hua   Finish your trip. Auntie Wang has no wisdom to deposit.

Sunny   Please, I just want to ask −

Wang Hua   I'll file a complaint if you don't stop harassing me!

Sunny   I don't know how to make decisions.

Wang Hua   Because you dropped out of Mother-in-Law University!

Sunny   What would I learn there, how to trim nose hair? You're right. You can't help me.

She starts to leave.

Wang Hua   Why was Auntie Wang's only child a son?

Sunny   Because you ate lots of lamb?

Wang Hua   Because I watched which women made boys and paid one of their husbands to fuck me. That was your last freebie. Next time you need an answer you're pulling me home like a donkey. The Auntie-Wang-Registered-Trademark Name-Brand-of-Decision is practical. It's a three-step process.

Sunny   What are the steps?

Wang Hua *sits regally in the cart, and motions for* **Sunny** *to take the handles. She does.*

Wang Hua Step one: pay attention. Look around. See everything. Not just what you want to see. Do not spread legs to handsome stranger – even if his skin smells like roses – if all his children are girls.

Sunny Step one: pay attention.

Wang Hua *claps her hands.* **Sunny** *pulls the cart.*

Wang Hua Step two: analyze information. If ugly man makes boys, ugly man is better than handsome girl-maker whose skin smells like roses – even if ugly man has needle dick – and moles in bad places.

Sunny *pauses.*

Sunny Step two: analyze information.

Wang Hua Step three: make decision. Based on analyzed information. Collected by paying attention.

Sunny Step three: make decision.

Wang Hua Handsome stranger makes girls. Mole-man needle-dick makes boys. Auntie Wang wants son. Hmm. Who should Auntie Wang fuck?

Sunny Needle-dick.

Wang Hua What is Auntie-Wang-Registered-Trademark-Name-Brand-of-Decision?

Sunny Pay attention. Analyze information. Make decision.

Wang Hua Again!

Sunny Pay attention. Analyze information. Make decision.

Wang Hua (*commanding* **Sunny** *to pull her*) Like donkey!

Sunny *pulls* **Wang Hua** *home.*

Sunny Pay attention. Analyze information. Make decision.

They exit.

Eight

The Great Hall of the People. **Sunny,** *dressed as a "model peasant" – braided hair, a handkerchief around her head, black cloth shoes – follows* **Artemis** *to a podium that has dozens of press microphones mounted on it.*

Artemis *(into microphone)*   Ladies and gentlemen, foreign dignitaries, members of the press and business community – welcome to the Great Hall of the People! The life of a migrant worker is fraught with struggle and great adversity.

Many leave impoverished homes in primitive villages and endure epic journeys in search of better lives for themselves and the ones they leave behind.

We have one of these heroes with us today. Here to introduce the world premiere of *Factory Girl*, a gripping new documentary about the hopes and dreams of young migrants, is nineteen-year-old Sunny Li, with her speech "Change, Challenge, Destiny."

She exits. **Sunny** *takes the podium. Dozens of camera flashes illuminate her face.*

Sunny *(into microphone)*   Ladies and gentlemen, esteemed foreigners, press and business people – good morning. My name is Sunny Li, and I am here to tell you how leaving the countryside to work in a city factory gave me the opportunity to transform my life and have some success.

Success. Back home – umm . . . back home it was – it was my job to grow food. Mostly vegetables. I was a bad farmer. My plants got sick. They dried up – or got moldy. And eaten – by stink bugs, and grasshoppers.

They didn't – they didn't grow the way vegetables should. My neighbor caught me yelling at my vegetables. She told me to stop being an idiot, brought over a wheelbarrow full of manure, and taught me how to feed vegetables – and surround them with straw – so they wouldn't burn in hot weather – or freeze in the winter. I became a good farmer but hated the countryside because I couldn't go to school. I knew if I didn't leave I'd marry a farmer and spend my life trying to make boy babies.

So I went to Shenzhen. To the factory. And . . . and I didn't like − I hated who I was. I thought the problem was me. I needed to change − so I went to night school − and studied self-improvement. I put marbles in my mouth. Bleach on my skin. Books on my head. Every month I tried a new hair color. One day − I was walking past a building covered in shiny windows, and saw the reflection of a city girl in it. It was me! Then two people from Beijing asked me for directions. That night I went to the top floor of a department store, got eyelash extensions and ate a hamburger in the food court. It felt like the beginning of success − even city people thought I was one of them.

I didn't know it wouldn't matter how much I looked like a city person − or how many people I tricked, because my ID card said peasant.

Artemis *enters and whispers into* **Sunny**'s *ear.*

Sunny   City people. They think they can burn through peasants. Like a − a natural resource. To them we're coal. We don't have the same rights, but . . . but we're supposed to make them rich.

Artemis *exits.*

Sunny   I want to say to the other migrants, that I am sorry for trying to be different. I thought − I thought it was the only way I could − save myself. And change my destiny.

Artemis *enters again, this time led by* **Qing Shu Min**.

Sunny   But destiny − it's not something one person can change. We have to work together and make − better growing conditions. For all of us. (*To* **Artemis**.) We need to have better dreams.

A beat, then **Artemis** *exits.* **Qing Shu Min** *approaches* **Sunny**.

Sunny   My section manager jumped out a factory window. There was a – petition by his body. Filled with hundreds of signatures. Every name was a protest. In the countryside there are always reasons to protest and people telling you not to protest.

Qing Shu Min *turns off* **Sunny***'s microphone.* **Gao Chen** *leads* **Artemis** *onstage.* **Artemis** *carries a cordless mic.*

Artemis   Thank you, Sunny. Ladies and gentlemen, please join us in the lobby for refreshments. The world premiere of *Factory Girl* will begin in thirty minutes

Sunny *steps away from the podium and speaks directly into the audience, over* **Artemis***. Dozens of camera flashes go off.*

Sunny   I want to say – to all my fellow migrant workers who are watching me right now – that I protest – and I ask you to protest with me. Ask – demand that you . . . that you get the same rights as people born in the city. If they say no . . . go on strike. Stop working. Make these demands every day – for a month. And – and if they still say no . . . if they still say no – go home.

Let city people – try to live – for a single day without us. Stop selling them food and digging out coal. Stop building their houses and sewing their clothes. Let the city people go hungry. Let them . . . walk – naked. On the street. Without shoes. And live in houses with – with broken windows and –

Lights shift. The podium, **Artemis** *and* **Qing Shu Min** *disappear.* **Sunny** *is backstage, more grounded and sure of herself than ever.*

Sunny *(dreamy)*   Chop off my arms – I can still strike. Hack off my legs – I can still walk. Rip out my heart – I will mysteriously recover. I can bathe in boiling oil and come out cleaner than I went in.

Gao Chen *places a black hood over* **Sunny***'s head. She doesn't struggle. He escorts her off.*

Nine

Li Han's *rural home.* **Li Han** *sits in a chair. There is a stapled document on his lap and an earphone in one ear.* **Qing Shu Min** *is in the next room, listening in on a headset. She holds a walkie-talkie in one hand.* **Gao Chen** *points a video camera at* **Li Han**. *It's recording.*

Li Han *(into camera)*   I . . . am . . . Li Han. The father of Sunny Li – the . . .

Qing Shu Min *(into walkie-talkie)*   – politically insane worker activist.

Li Han   Politically insane worker activist.

Qing Shu Min   Focus.

Li Han   I have been told that some – some –

Qing Shu Min *(interrupting)*   Uninformed internet bloggers.

Li Han   – people believe Sunny's actions were motivated by the –

Qing Shu Min *(interrupting)*   Untimely death.

Li Han   – by what happened to my brother, Li Chen. When he took part in –

Qing Shu Min *(interrupting)*   A counter-revolutionary riot.

Li Han   – student demonstrations – during the –

Qing Shu Min   – period of   **Li Han**   – eighty-nine
political turmoil.   democracy movement.

Li Han   At home Sunny was an obedient girl who never caused trouble. Only when she went to the factory and was exposed to . . . political agitators and – urban intellectuals did her –

Qing Shu Min *(interrupting)*   Mental illness.

Li Han   – problems develop. I am not suited to care for Sunny's illness. So . . . so I am relinquishing Sunny's guardianship to the state. So she can . . . receive the – medical attention she needs to recover from her condition and become a productive member of society.

Qing Shu Min   Sign the papers, then apologize to the country.

Li Han *takes the pen and signs the document on his lap. He bows towards the camera.*

Li Han   Forgive me for raising a Bad Element.

Qing Shu Min *takes out a large envelope stuffed full of one-hundred yuan notes and offers it to* **Li Han***.*

Qing Shu Min   By accepting this compensation you agree not to sue the factory.

Li Han   She's just a girl.

Qing Shu Min   It's time to forget the past and face a brighter future. You deserve a chance at happiness. Don't you agree?

Li Han *takes the money.* **Pete** *enters.*

Pete   Where is she?

Li Han   Shut up!

Pete   Where's Sunny?

Qing Shu Min   Your sister is sick. There's a hospital in Beijing where she'll get the medical care that she needs.

Pete   She's not sick.

Qing Shu Min   Forget about your sister. Improve yourself, and life for your father.

Pete *spits in* **Qing Shu Min***'s face.* **Gao Chen** *grabs him.* **Li Han** *falls to his knees.*

Li Han   Forgive him – I beg you – he's all I have left –

Qing Shu Min *takes out a handkerchief and meticulously wipes her face.*

Qing Shu Min   Keep an eye on your son. Given your family's history, mental illness could be hereditary.

Qing Shu Min *and* **Gao Chen** *exit.* **Li Han** *exits to the pigeon loft.* **Pete** *exits the house.*

Ten

Beijing Ankang Psychiatric Hospital. **Sunny** *sits on a metal chair in an otherwise empty space, dressed in dirty white pajamas. Months of torture and medication have made it difficult to recognize names and faces. Her body is there, her mind nearly destroyed. Her arms, legs and face are covered in bruises. For the entire scene, her head dangles limply to the side, her mouth hangs open and her bulging eyes stare vacantly at the ceiling.* **Pete** *enters, dressed in a blue janitor's uniform.*

Pete   Sunny?

No response from **Sunny**.

Pete   Sunny, it's me. Can you hear me?

Sunny   . . .

Pete   I was worried you might not recognize me because of all the – (*He looks around, suddenly fearful.*)   You know who I am. You recognize me. Don't you?

Sunny   . . .

Pete   I got a job as a janitor so I can see you whenever I want. I had to go to the labor market every day for three months. But I'm here now. Are you happy to see me?

Sunny   . . .

Pete   Last month I met a man who used to perform Monkey King in tea houses – look what he's taught me –

He executes a sequence of fluttering, staggering movements – the Drunken Monkey sequence, from Peking Opera.

Pete   That's 'Drunken Monkey.' I learned it for you. (*Still moving.*) Monkey moves like this after getting drunk on the wine of immortality he steals from the Emperor of Heaven. Remember? They sentence him to death, but when they try to chop off his head the blade breaks, and the fire they burn him with –

Sunny (*interrupting*)   Ahhannngeeeeehmeeee.

Pete   What?

Sunny   . . .

Pete   The fire they burn him with tickles. Even the golden arrows can't pierce his skin.

Sunny   Aaaange me.

Pete   Aaange you?

Sunny   Change me!

Pete   Change you? Into what?

Sunny *tries to cup her hands together, referencing a gesture she knows* **Pete** *will understand.* **Pete** *shows* **Sunny** *his cell phone and plays a video excerpt of her speech.*

Pete   You're a hero. A peasant hero. Your speech is on the internet. Millions of people watched it and guess what? All the workers in our factory went on strike. Other places too – all over. Even miners and construction workers heard you. Everything's stopped.

Sunny   . . .

Pete   Two months ago the factories closed and now all the pollution is gone. A week ago there was rain – now the skies are bluer than anyone can remember. Last night in Beijing you could even see stars. The city slickers were scared – they had never seen such a bright sky. They thought the stars were American missiles coming to wage World War Three on us.

Sunny   . . .

Pete   Peasants are going back to the countryside to make their own jobs, start their own schools and take care of each other. It's the Sunshine Revolution! After you! The countryside had an election to choose a new leader. There was no corruption, murders or bribes – and guess who they chose?

Sunny . . .

Pete   You're Chairlady Sunny, and until we figure out a perfect society and get rid of money your face will be on all the bills. It's only an honorary title because people will rule themselves, but guess what they asked me give you –

Pete *exits and returns with an office chair, the kind that rolls and swivels.*

Pete   Tadaaa!

Pete *lifts* **Sunny** *and moves her to the office chair. She whimpers, her body jerks and spasms, then comes to stillness when he sets her down.*

Pete   The Citizens of the Countryside have authorized me to remove you from this hospital so you can begin your new office position.

Sunny   . . .

Pete *spins* **Sunny** *in the chair. He pushes the chair and* **Sunny** *through the space. Faster and faster, in spirals.* **Sunny** *remains limp and motionless.*

Pete   Ladies and gentlemen, presenting the face of the Sunshine Revolution, Chairlady Sunny! Whee!

They come to a stop. **Sunny** *is the same as before.*

Sunny (*begging*)   Change me.

Long silence, as **Pete** *struggles with her request.*

Pete   Later, as punishment for making outrageous claims and trying to cross the universe in one leap, Buddha made a Magic Mountain and trapped Monkey in it. He would have been stuck there, but the Goddess of Mercy obtained Monkey's release, so he could travel to Western Paradise and receive the Great Teachings.

Sunny   . . .

Pete   Imagine everything you don't need flying out your fingers and toes. Back into the dirt and sky. When you open your eyes, your life will be wide open with possibility. It will be beautiful and blank.

Sunny   . . .

Pete   Let go of your past. Let everything fade away. Face your future with clear eyes and a strong body. Are you ready?

Sunny (*whispers*)   Change me.

Pete *claps his hands together as if to perform the Spell of Seventy-Two Transformations,*

Pete   Take a deep breath.

They do this together.

Now, change.

He clamps his hands over **Sunny***'s nose and mouth, suffocating her. He holds her as her body rebels, thrashes, pleads and struggles for life – until she goes limp, and collapses into him.* **Pete** *exits.* **Sunny** *remains in the chair, her eyes still open.*

A long, silent, stillness.

End of Play.

Background

BOOKS

Factory Girls: From Village to City in a Changing China, by Leslie T. Chang.

Message from an Unknown Chinese Mother: Stories of Loss and Love, by Xinran.

Laogai: The Machinery of Repression in China, cd. Nan Richardson.

The Corpsewalker – Real Life Stories: China from the Bottom Up, by Liao Yi Wu.

Hungry Ghosts: Mao's Secret Famine, by Jasper Becker.

Wild Grass: Three Stories of Change in Modern China, by Ian Johnson.

Ai Weiwei's Blog: Writings, Interviews, and Digital Rants, 2006–2009, by Ai Weiwei.

FILM AND TELEVISION

Chinese Dreamers, short documentary dir. Sharon Lovell.

Up the Yangtze, documentary dir. Yung Chang.

Last Train Home, documentary dir. Lixin Fan.

Not One Less, drama film dir. Zhang Yimou.

24 City, film dir. Jia Zhangke.

The People's Republic of Capitalism, Discovery Channel miniseries, dir. Ted Koppel.

Taiwan to the World: The Pigeon Game, National Geographic miniseries.

WEBSITES

The Ministry of Tofu: http://www.ministryoftofu.com

Charter 08 for Reform and Democracy in China: http://www.charter08.eu/2.html

2012 Statement by Yu Jie, Charter 08 co-author: http://www.hrichina.org/content/5778

Laogai Research Foundation: http://www.laogai.org

China Digital Times: http://chinadigitaltimes.net

China Labor Watch: http://www.chinalaborwatch.org

Afterword

Frances Ya-Chu Cowhig's *The World of Extreme Happiness* begins as Li Han, a coal miner in rural China and the father of the play's principle protagonist, describes a dream. Xin Xin, who the audience member is led to believe is a prostitute, comes to his bed and sits on his face. While "savoring her warmth on my skin," Li Han is surprised to find "something hot and gooey slide down my cheek." When he realizes that Xin Xin has "laid a turd between my eyes," instead of responding with revulsion, he describes it as "salty, and sweet. Like tofu, fermented with black beans." There is an uncomfortable disconnect for the audience member, being asked to imagine a seemingly abject occurrence (human feces falling onto one's face and into an open mouth) as potentially nourishing. Li Han's friend, Ran Feng, interprets the dream thus: "You accepted shit into your mouth and digested it." A few moments later we learn that Xin Xin is not, in fact, a woman, but one of Li Han's beloved racing pigeons. While his fecophilic dream may seem no less unsettling to some in the audience, Li Han's metaphor of fermented tofu with black beans still asks us to imagine "shit" as something that is not only digestible, but potentially delicious.

Ran Feng's explanation of Li Han's dream seems to resonate with the Ai Weiwei quote Cowhig chose as an epigram to this edition of the play. In this sense, the "people" have come to swallow shit ("the deceptions of culture") and learned to digest it as they've "abandoned their rights and responsibilities." But just as Xin Xin's identity is unstable in the opening scene (is she a prostitute, or a bird?), what it is that constitutes "the people" and/or the object of criticism in Cowhig's play is no more stable. Are we to understand "the people" as the eponymous source of power in the People's Republic of China (PRC), as "the people" of US-style constitutional democracy, the people in the audience, or the specific people onstage in front of us? Perhaps more important is the question of what or who is the source of the "shit" that the people happily digest? In these notes I will open up a few possibilities for approaching these questions.

The play follows Sunny, Li Han's daughter, after she is born into rural poverty in 1992. Sunny is discarded and left to die in a garbage can when her gender is revealed as female at birth. Surviving against the odds, she grows up and leaves her home for the bustling urban center in Shenzhen to find work in a factory. There, Sunny is caught up in a web of corporate and political intrigue. Due in part to her aspirations to climb the corporate ladder and become a self-made success, Sunny becomes a pawn in a transnational company's cynical public relations campaign, resulting in her utter destruction.

The play is set between 1992 and 2012, an era of extraordinary transformation that arguably began with the brutal government and military crackdown on the 1989 Democracy Movement. Popular Western conceptions of June 4th, 1989 often frame it as a pro-Western-style democracy uprising against the staunch authoritarianism of the Chinese Communist state. But the 1989 protests were a complex constellation of grievances that were partially responding to the state's use of anti-democratic measures to forward anti-socialist reforms in pursuit of then President Deng Xiaoping's newly articulated "socialist market economy." Indeed, as many cultural critics have since observed, many of the students were motivated by criticism of the rampant corruption fostered by capitalist reforms as well as by opposition to the increased privatization of formerly worker-controlled and stated-owned industry. In other words, students were not only protesting for democratic reform but in some cases simultaneously protesting against the state's increasingly capitalist policies.[1]

The specter of the June 4th massacre in Tiananmen Square hangs heavily over *The World of Extreme Happiness*, most notably in the form of Li Han's brother, who we learn was killed as a protester in Beijing. But it is not the past that most compels Cowhig's characters so much as the promise of the future. That Sunny is born in 1992 is important. After a few years of internal instability following the events of 1989, the PRC shifted to governance by what cultural critic Xudong Zhang describes as the pro-market reform, "bureaucratic and technocratic elite, itself the biggest beneficiary of Reform policies."[2] In 1990 and 1991, stock exchanges were opened in Shanghai and Shenzhen, respectively. Deng Xiaoping, who handed the Presidency over to Jiang Zemin in 1989, publicly re-emerged in 1992 (the year of Sunny's birth) to promote his vision of pro-market reform. By 1997, with the support of the Fifteenth Congress of the Chinese Communist Party, President Jiang publicly endorsed a shareholding system that would further facilitate the privatization of state-owned enterprises in an increasing shift towards capitalist reforms.

Named Sunny, our heroine thus embodies the dawn of this New Era in Chinese politics. She is literally rescued from the garbage bin of the past and her story is significant of a new kind of ideal Chinese subject, with a self-sacrificing, entrepreneurial, pro-market spirit. Her journey from rural China to the bustling urban center of Shenzhen might then be understood as reflective of the shift from the peasant proletarianism of the Maoist era to the pro-market ideology of the new one. In this sense, the play is much more than a simple critique of the PRC. Rather, it is a nuanced meditation on labor and life in the post-Tiananmen period whereby, as Zhang remarks, "the central political tension in Chinese society today is not so much the discrepancy between a Communist government and a market environment – since the two have already effected a corporate-style merger – but rather an intensifying conflict between this interest group's rational self-interest and its unchecked power and corruption, which put it in direct confrontation with society at large."[3]

To this end, the setting of the play, in Shenzhen, is significant. As the owner of the factory where Sunny finds employment explains, Shenzhen is one of China's Special Economic Zones (SEZs). Located largely along China's eastern border, SEZs are defined as spaces that are exempt from a range of the PRC's laws and regulations in order, in the words of the Fifth

Congress, to "encourage foreign citizens . . . to set up factories and establish enterprises and other undertakings."[4] SEZs are largely reliant upon migrant labor from rural areas and, as anthropologist Aihwa Ong observes, "zone workers are considered peasants unprotected by China's labor laws and are not entitled to social benefits due workers elsewhere in the country."[5] What makes SEZs unique is thus the fact that they are effectively outside of what many in the West refer to as the administrative state of "Communist China." They are instead capitalist zones that function under direct control of the central Chinese government. The result is that, as in similarly constituted free-trade zones in places such as Indonesia, "workers are denied the most basic of social protections and are generally unshielded from the onslaught of capital while remaining vulnerable to the state's repressive apparatus."[6] These are precisely the conditions that result in Sunny's destruction.

That the exploitative conditions inside of SEZs were established with the explicit goal of attracting foreign capital undermines any attempt to read *The World of Extreme Happiness* as a strict critique of the PRC's governing policies insofar as global circuits of production and consumption are equally culpable. Returning to my question about what is the "source" of the abject filth that "the people" are willing to swallow, we find a monster with two heads: the repressive apparatuses of the central Chinese state *and* the economic conditions produced by transnational capitalism. The regime of capitalist exploitation that structures labor conditions within factories in Shenzhen is present throughout the play and Cowhig is careful to remind us that Western economic ideology, investment, *and* consumption are prime structuring factors in this model of development. For example, factory owner James Lin and business executive Artemis Chang are literal embodiments of the New Era's marriage to Western market reforms. They have taken recognizably Western names and, indeed, Artemis (the daughter of accused counter-revolutionaries) is neatly representative of the new economic elite in China. Educated at Harvard and a shining example of global cosmopolitanism,

Artemis wants nothing more than to place the past under erasure, embracing a vulgar capitalist ideology of selfishness and the pursuit of wealth: "There are only two roads to walk down . . . You can see the truth – and always be in pain. Or we can look away and be rich. And safe. And happy." But look away from what?

Early in the play, as James and Artemis discuss a "spate of worker suicides" at Lin's factory, Chang suggests that Lin "Follow the example of Fox-Conn and ask them to sign a no-suicide pledge." Fox-Conn is a multi-national Taiwanese owned corporation responsible for the manufacture of many popular commodities including Apple's iPhone and iPad. In recent years, Fox-Conn has become notorious for its exploitation and abuse of laborers in its Shenzhen factory. Drawing a subtle connection between the horrors and abuses that structure the world of the fictional factory in the play and the very real Fox-Conn, Cowhig is gently asking the audience to look towards and at the exploitative labor conditions that are rendered invisible in the final commodity form of the popular electronics that line our pockets.

And if we are quick to indict the Chinese government for using brutal tactics to maintain this system of production, the play is unwilling to allow consumers to shirk responsibility for our role in these practices. This is most apparent when Artemis complains about the "violent tactics" of the Chinese government to policewoman Qing Shu Min. To this, Qing wryly quips, "Why would we change when everyone wants to sleep with us just the way we are?" Having made the link between Fox-Conn, the Western media, and Western consumers earlier in the play, this exchange is a subtle indictment of the audience member's own complicity with and relationship to the violence that we see carried out on stage. Qing deploys a sexual metaphor, which also invites us to think back to Li Han's dream and question what it is that we've been willing to "look away" from in order to continue "sleeping" with a regime that allows us to consume and digest the sweet and salty "shit" that surges forth from Shenzhen's factories.

If both capitalism and state repression are targeted by Cowhig's narrative, part of what makes *The World of Extreme Happiness* so compelling is the author's unwillingness to relinquish Sunny's own agency in her story. Although she is crafted to be sympathetic and even likeable, she's hardly uncompromised. Perhaps more than any other character in the play, Sunny embraces the ideology of self-promotion and corporate ambition. With resonances of Artemis' personal history, it is not difficult to imagine Sunny as a younger version of Chang. Throughout the play Sunny literally speaks in the catchphrases of capitalist opportunism, becoming an enthusiastic protégé of Mr. Destiny's smoke-and-mirror self-help classes. At one point, she defines her desire for class mobility in relatively petty terms: once she makes her fortune she wants to "go back to the countryside and laugh at everyone who's still poor . . . and living in dirt." Her ambition leads her to betray her best friend and her pettiness results in an act of cruelty against her father that, though matched by his own callous treatment of his children, is no less horrifying to watch. In fact, Sunny only truly becomes a heroine in the final instance, when she performs a public account of the horrible conditions experienced by the working masses in the New Era.

If Sunny is significant of the dawning hope of the New Era in China, her death might then be understood as the loss of a hope that was little more than a lie. In the final sequence, she is destroyed, mentally and physically, by the state's violent response to her revolutionary action. But in this last scene Cowhig offers us a new hope in the form of a utopian vision of a changed and better world. The world of happiness that we imagine as the "Sunshine Revolution" is not one of unrestrained free-market entrepreneurialism or state-based repression. Rather, Sunny's brother Pete tells the story of a world in which the people collectively and spontaneously reject the filth that they have been digesting in order to rise up against the forces that have appropriated the people's name, and thus their constituent power. Against capitalism's false assurances of individual enrichment, and against the authoritarianism of the Chinese central government, Pete allows Sunny (and by extension, the audience) to imagine a "perfect society" built on the empowerment of the masses, true democracy, liberty, and the promise of the collective struggle for justice. By allowing us to imagine this promise, we are assured that such a world is possible. In what he does next, Pete reminds us of the painful gap that we must bridge between that world and this one.

Joshua Takano Chambers-Letson
Northwestern University

1. For more, see: Xudong Zhang, ed., *Whither China: Intellectual Politics in Contemporary China* (Durham, NC: Duke University Press, 2001).

2. Xudong Zhang, "The Making of the Post-Tiananmen Intellectual Field: A Critical Overview," in *Whither China: Intellectual Politics in Contemporary China*, ed. Xudong Zhang (Durham, NC: Duke University Press, 2001), 7.

3. Ibid.

4. Fifth National People's Congress, "Regulations on Special Economic Zones in Guangdong Province." Available at: www.novexcn.com/guangdong_regs_on_sez.html, accessed September 7, 2013.

5. Aihwa Ong, *Neoliberalism as Exception: Mutations in Citizenship and Sovereignty* (Durham, NC: Duke University Press, 2006), 106.

6. Aihwa Ong, *Flexible Citizenship: The Cultural Logics of Transnationality* (Durham, NC: Duke University Press, 1999), 224.